DATE			

Issue Voting and Party Realignment

Issue
Voting
and
Party
Realignment

DONALD S. STRONG

THE UNIVERSITY OF ALABAMA PRESS
University, Alabama

JK
1967
S78

```
Library of Congress Cataloging in Publication Data
```

Strong, Donald Stuart, 1912-
  Issue voting and party realignment.

  Includes bibliographical references and index.
  1. Voting—United States—Addresses, essays,
  lectures.
2. Voting research—United States—Addresses, essays,
lectures. 3. Party affiliation—United States—
Addresses, essays, lectures. I. Title.
JK1967.S78   324'.2   77-1087
ISBN 0-8173-4836-0
ISBN 0-8173-4837-9 pbk.

Contents

Preface

These chapters were prepared originally as the annual lectures delivered to the students in the Southern Regional Training Program, a cooperative arrangement for graduate study in Public Administration sponsored by the Universities of Alabama, Tennessee, and Kentucky. The primary interest of these students is to explore the mysteries of budgeting, personnel, and organization theory and to acquire a command of the esoteric vocabularies in these fields. Hence, these lectures were presented at a level suitable for the non-specialist. Their purpose is to set forth the changing views of the experts on American voting behavior that have taken place over the last twenty-five years. The author's attempt has been to set forth in basic English both the conventional wisdom and the departures therefrom in the hope that this study may be of value in introducing alert undergraduates to the voluminous literature in this area.

D.S.S.

Issue Voting and Party Realignment

One

CAN ISSUE-CONSCIOUS VOTERS

SAVE THE REPUBLIC?

A classic question in democratic theory is how smart one expects the voter to be. If one endorses the mandate theory, he assumes that the voters transmit to their elected officials a specific policy program. The only responsibility left to the officials is to carry out these wishes. At the other end of the spectrum is the position attributed—if I am not mistaken—to Aristotle. The average man may not know how to construct a good house, but after living in it, he knows whether or not it is a sound dwelling

1

and keeps out the weather. Similarly the voters are
not expected to devise a program for their salvation,
but, when they feel they are being governed poorly,
they have the invaluable privilege of voting out one
set of rulers and trying another set. American
folklore probably leans closer to the mandate
theory. This is a difficult and exacting role to give
the voter, and it frequently leads to disillusionment
and cynicism. It is all too easy to demonstrate that
the average person is more interested in watching
his television than in studying the qualifications of
the candidates for the forty-odd offices on the
Alabama Democratic primary ballot and then
observing the behavior of the persons eventually
elected.

Our knowledge of what goes on inside the head of
a voter is restricted almost exclusively to national
politics. An early study, one that is now almost
American intellectual history, examined the 1940
presidential election in Erie County, Ohio, and attributed the voter's decision to something close to
demographic determinism.[1] Once you know various
demographic details about a person, your prediction
of how he will vote will be accurate most of the time.
As a person is, so he thinks. One might argue that
when a person voted in harmony with his social
status he was behaving in a rational manner. The
71 percent of those in the upper-economic level who
voted for Republican Wendell Willkie may have
perceived their economic interest. Yet the noneconomic determinants like religion, age, or

urban-rural residence are not convincing instances of rationality. Rural dwellers may well have voted on the basis of a Civil War tradition, and there was no issue that would have impelled a Catholic to support F.D.R. Voters read or listened to anything that supported their views; they avoided any propaganda that might change their minds.

More nearly a classic and somewhat more relevant to the voter's perception of issues is the article appearing in the June, 1960, *American Political Science Review* entitled "Issue Conflict and Consensus among Party Leaders and Followers."[2] A mail questionnaire dealing with 24 important issues was sent to all the delegates to both the Republican and Democratic conventions of 1956. In January, 1958 the Gallup organization distributed the same questionnaire to 2,918 adult voters. Each respondent was asked whether he thought that the level of government support for each issue should be increased, decreased, or remain as it is. Let us focus our attention on the citizen responses. The chief finding of the study was that the policy preferences of voters in the two parties were not far apart. An interesting sidelight was that Democratic voters, Republican voters, and Democratic leaders were all in rather close agreement. All three groups showed only small differences in scores on whether government should increase, decrease, or stand pat on the 24 selected activities. By contrast, Republican leaders stood alone and apart, generally agreed among themselves in their approval or disapproval on what government should be doing. (It should be noted that no respondents, either delegates or rank-and-file, were subjected to tests as to the adequacy of their knowledge of what government was actually doing about slum clearance or anything else.) The primary finding was that Americans of both parties agreed on what government should do—save only the Republican leaders. Voters demonstrated an ability to react to issues questions, but the issue preferences of the two groups of voters were remarkably similar.

Yet the true fount of conventional wisdom on this subject is Angus Campbell *et al, The American Voter,*[3] and to it we must now direct our attention. (Incidentally the term "conventional wisdom" is not employed here in a patronizing sense. Many of us who are still on the hoof were not doing anything particularly exciting when Campbell and his Survey Research Group were pioneering in their studies.) Campbell and associates stressed the idea of asking respondents whether they were Democrats, Republicans, or Independents. He then pressed the partisans as to whether they regarded themselves as strong or weak Democrats or Republicans. If Independents, did they lean toward the Democrats or the Republicans, or were they strictly Independent? Campbell then applied three separate tests to discern both the level of information possessed by voters and their thought processes. The first test of voter information dealt with the familiarity with public issues. Voters were questioned concerning a series of sixteen issues dating back to the New Deal era or slightly later. Questions dealt with specific issues such as public power, the Taft-Hartley Act, Fair Employment, etc. Three rather exacting criteria were set up. First, the respondent must grasp the issue to some degree; he must have some vague idea of what it is all about. Secondly, he must have some feeling about the issue; is it a good idea, or is it the worst thing that ever happened to the country? Thirdly, he must believe that one party represents the position on the issue better than the other party does, although his impression may be erroneous. For instance, of those who understood the general idea of public electric power and had some feeling about the matter, twenty-five percent regarded it as an issue that the Republican party favored. The conclusion was that, on the sixteen issues which respondents grasped to some degree and had feelings about, the percent perceiving party differences ranged from as low as eighteen up to only thirty-six.

Yet perhaps this type of test is too exacting for the average American. After all, it is somewhat of a current events test that one might take after having read the same news magazine for six months. Maybe the voters think in the more general terms of attitude or ideology. They may move toward the left or toward the right, impelled by questions of ideology even though they are poorly informed on specific issues. At this point Campbell draws a distinction between the expressions *attitude structure* and an *ideology*. An attitude structure consists merely of two or more beliefs that are logically related. For example, a person might believe in both Old Age Insurance and Medicare. Both programs vest in the government activities that have in earlier periods of history been assumed by individuals. By contrast an ideology is defined as an elaborate, closely woven, and far-reaching structure of attitudes. An ideology is not identical with a political philosophy; rather it is a watered-down version of one—a popularized version.

The authors found it was possible to do only a minimal amount of scaling of attitude structure because attitudes on most issues simply did not scale. There is only a moderate distinction between parties on what the authors refer to as the social-welfare scale. Admittedly, Republicans turn out to be somewhat more conservative than Democrats, but a much greater difference is found between persons of varying levels of education, which the authors use as a measure of class status. The well-educated, whether Republicans or Democrats, have less enthusiasm for what is measured by the social-welfare scale than poorly educated members of both parties, who score higher on the scale. Seemingly we are measuring primitive self-interest, not party philosophy.

Finally, the authors try bravely to discover whether voters think in ideological terms. Here their method consists in recording the answers to these open-ended questions: "Is there anything you particularly like about the Democrats?" and "Is there anything you particularly dislike about the Democrats?" followed by corresponding questions about the Republicans. An extremely small percentage of voters occasionally used words like "liberal" or "rightist," but the largest percentage simply made some vague remarks about the advancement of some particular interest group or made some generalized reference to the nature of the times. The inescapable conclusion is that Campbell's American voters were poorly informed about specific issues, were not given to holding attitudes that were logically interrelated, and most certainly did not think in ideological terms. The voter did not come through as at all issue-oriented. The main determinant of presidential choice was party identification, that is, party loyalty.

Support for this unflattering view of the voter had earlier been provided by another well-known study. Published in 1954 and written by Berelson, Lazarsfeld, and McPhee, it was entitled *Voting*.[4] The locale of their study was Elmira, New York. One may summarize their conclusion about the 1948 election with outrageous brevity in the following manner. In that community there were two well-defined parties whose members were committed to support the party's nominee and not at all disposed to defect. The sides were nearly evenly matched. Voters, if not well-informed, at least exposed themselves to considerable propaganda, each from his own side. The election was then decided by a minority of citizens who voted only occasionally, had only the mildest interest in politics, and possessed almost no information on the subject. So the authors reached the even more pessimistic conclusion that presidential elections were decided by the most ignorant and the most indifferent voters.

Happily the academic world was not forced to wallow forever in pessimism. The idea that voters were no fools was championed by the late V. O. Key in his posthumously published *The Responsible Electorate*.[5] Key's procedure was to contact the Gallup polling organization and inventory the data that they had collected for the elections 1936–1960, both inclusive. Gallup had not confined his questioning to the issue of for whom the respondent intended to vote. For example, in 1936, each respondent was also asked whether he favored the compulsory old-age insurance plan, plus several other questions on issues of that era. In all subsequent elections, questions of contemporary interest were raised, and respondents were asked whether they approved or disapproved of the government's policy. On this basis all respondents were classified into standpatters, switchers, and new voters. A *standpatter* was a voter who had supported the same party in two consecutive elections. Information was limited to these two consecutive elections because all Gallup asked about this matter was how the voter intended to vote and how he had voted in the preceding election. A *switcher* was a voter who voted for different parties in two consecutive elections.

Now in a world of issue-conscious voters, only a small percent of 1932 Democrats who switched to the Republicans in 1936 would favor the old-age insurance plan. On the other hand, it would be quite rational for a much larger percentage of 1932 Democrats opposed to the old-age insurance plan to switch to the Republicans in 1936. In this example our statistical universe consists of 1932 supporters of Franklin Roosevelt, and of course, the old-age insurance plan was introduced by the Democratic administration between the two elections.

The term *new voter* is a more ambiguous one since it means anyone who had not voted in the preceding election whether because of ineligibility or indifference. He was not necessarily a youthful first voter. Regardless of the election or the issue, the voters displayed an impressive degree of consistency. For instance, in 1952, this question was put to the respondents: "In labor disputes in the last two or three years, have your sympathies been in general on the side of the unions or on the side of the companies?" Of all the 1948 Democrats who sympathized with the companies, 47 percent switched to the Republicans; whereas only 16 percent of those who sympathized with the unions made the switch. Of all the new voters who voted Republican, 72% sympathized with the companies.

In a whole series of questions covering nearly three decades there was the same demonstration of a high percentage of citizens voting in harmony with their views on issues. Those who favored the acts of the administration during the preceding four years tended to be standpatters, whereas a high percentage of those disapproving the administration's actions switched.

Key attacked also the idea that the switchers were a less informed and less desirable type of voter. One might note that his definition of a switcher is not identical with the occasional voter discussed in the Berelson volume. In maintaining this argument, Key was more persuasive for the election of 1952 than for the election of 1960. In the election of 1952 he demonstrated that the average level of education of switchers did not differ significantly from those of the standpatters. Moreover, the switchers contained no higher proportion of persons with "no opinion" than did the standpatters of both parties. Nor do switchers have a lower level of interest in politics if we may believe the self-rating scale asking, "Generally speaking, how much interest would you say you have in politics—a great deal, fair amount, only a little, or no interest at all?" Differences between the two groups were unimpressive. Another question read: "How much thought have you given to the coming November election—quite a lot, or only a little?" The upshot of the analysis is that the switchers in both directions do not differ materially in the average amount of thought given the election from the standpatters whom they join. The most impressive difference turns up among the new voters, that is, those who had not voted at the preceding election. This group produces a much higher percentage who had given no thought or "only a little." It might be well to remember that Key's findings for 1960 along this line were not quite so persuasive.

Another champion of voter awareness of issues is Gerald M. Pomper writing in the June, 1972 issue of the *American Political Science Review*.[6] Pomper dealt with the six specific policy questions that have been asked consistently by the Michigan Survey Research Center of its sample in every election since 1956. (In 1956 and in other years more than six questions were asked, but only six questions have been asked consistently in all subsequent elections.) Pomper analyzes, first, the relationship between these issue preferences and party identification. In three separate tests employed by Pomper the issues presented were Federal Aid to Education, Medical Care, Job Guarantee, Fair Employment, School Integration, and Foreign Aid. The time period covered was the four presidential elections 1956–1968. Respondents are grouped in a continuum extending from strong Democrats to strong Republicans. In the first test, the question put to them is their personal preference with respect to public policy, and the statistic reported is the percentage taking the liberal position, that is, in favor of federal government action. For 1956, the finding, in harmony with *The American Voter,* is that issue preference was practically unrelated to party identification. A linear relationship existed only on the issue of Medical Care. By 1968, a linear relationship existed essentially on all issues except Foreign Aid. For example, strong Democrats were more favorable to Federal Aid to Education than were weak Democrats, and the progression continued down through strong Republicans, who were least enthusiastic on the issue.

A second change is evident in terms of the increasing percentage of voters perceiving party differences regardless of their own policy preferences. American voters have been assured from time to time that there is not a dime's worth of difference between the parties. The Pomper piece offers evidence that an increasing number of voters perceive party differences on various issues. "In 1956, the Survey Research Center found little awareness of differences. It subjected its respondents to a series of questions on each policy question. It eliminated those who had no interest in, or opinion on an issue, as well as those who, holding an opinion on the issue, could not decide if 'the government is going too far, doing less than it should, or what'?"[7] Campbell found that this latter question usually eliminated more respondents than the query on the issue itself. Those who were left after the multiple screening were then asked whether there was a difference between the parties. In 1956 this relatively knowledgeable group found rather little distinction between the parties on most issues, yet in 1960 and 1964, in five out of six issues (Foreign Aid being the only exception) respondents saw a greater difference between the parties than in the Eisenhower era. It was the strong Republicans and

the strong Democrats that had the clearest perception of party differences, as logically should be the
case.

Possibly of more basic importance is the third
finding, namely, that there was a substantial
agreement as to which party in a general sense was
the most liberal or took the most activist position.
As early as 1956, the Democrats regarded their
party as more liberal, but by 1964 and 1968 Republicans and Independents also perceived it as the
more liberal party, and an even higher percentage
of Democrats attributed the greater degree of
liberalism to their party.

Pomper, seeking to explain the reasons for the
change, sets up and then rejects his first two
hypotheses. One of them is the impact of age. He
hypothesizes that younger, more ideologically at-
tuned voters may have replaced older and less sensi-
tive electors. Respondents in the age grouping used
in the 1956 survey are compared to cohorts four,
eight, and twelve years older in the following three
elections. Although there was a somewhat greater
degree of change among the younger groups, there
was substantial change among all groups, particularly for the election of 1964.

Years of education might be an alternative explanation. Since the average level of schooling has
increased considerably in the nation in this
twelve-year period, one might expect to find a
greater degree of perception among the increasingly
large number of college alumni.

"In fact the disparities in perceptions among per-

sons of varying schooling have tended to lessen,
particularly in regard to identifying the Democrats
as the liberal party. This effect was most marked in
the 1964 campaign; in that year, on every issue,
respondents with only a grade-school education
were clearer in their perceptions of the parties than
college graduates had been in 1956."[8] As we shall
note later, writers are not unanimous on the impact
of education. Pomper does not conclude with an
assault on *The American Voter*. He believes that the
volume reported accurately the situation in the
Eisenhower era and that it is the voters who have
changed. The harshest thing he says of *The American Voter* is that it is "time-bound." This is an adjective used by academicians when they believe that
an author has generalized or universalized from
data taken at a particular period of history. In this
sense, Pomper is less critical than Key who believed
he had demonstrated that even the voters of the
1950s were more issue-conscious than *The American Voter* found them.

Pomper's treatment ends with the 1968 election.
A valuable source of information on the 1972 elec-
tion is a lengthy mimeographed piece entitled, "A
Majority Party in Disarray: Policy Polarization in
the 1972 Election," authored by Arthur H. Miller,
Warren E. Miller, Alden S. Raine, and Thad A.
Brown, all of the Center for Political Studies at the
University of Michigan. The immediate relevance
of the study is that it indicates a continuation of a
very real issue-consciousness in the 1972 election.

The data came from the 1972 poll by the Survey Research Center. A variety of questions are put to respondents. One category might be described as non-economic. It includes attitudes on the Vietnam War, marijuana, campus unrest, and amnesty for draft evaders. Two questions deal with race: minorities and busing. Five other issues— presumably economic—were also raised. The questions were phrased so that the respondent's answer could be classified left, center, or right. The five issues were handled on this basis but also converted into a liberal-conservative scale which in turn had its left, center, and right divisions. The table also covers presidential primaries; one column lists the answers of McGovern voters; the second, those of all other Democratic primary candidates. For the November election there are columns of Democrats Voting for McGovern, Democrats Voting for Nixon, All Democrats, All McGovern Voters. Policy divisions among these categories were abundantly clear. Persons voting for Nixon ended up in the right-hand category in almost all cases save in a few instances where they fell in the center. By contrast, persons voting for McGovern in November were much more likely to give answers putting the majority of them in the left category, with a few in the center. An even more instructive contrast is that of the attitudes of Democrats voting for McGovern with that of Democrats voting for Nixon. Note that we are talking here in terms of Democratic identifiers. Contrasts were evident throughout the an-

swers to the series of questions. Democrats voting
for McGovern were twice as dovish on Vietnam,
three times more sympathetic toward amnesty and
campus unrest. They were twice as favorable to the
left position on minorities and more than three
times as prone to fall into the left category on the
liberal-conservative issue. The Democratic identifiers voting for Nixon in November were extremely close in attitude to the entire universe of
Nixon voters, of which they were, of course, a part.
McGovern received the support of 58% of Democratic identifiers. If we follow the type of reasoning
advanced by Key in *The Responsible Electorate,* it
follows that those Democratic identifiers who took
positions similar to the majority of Nixon voters and
then defected to Nixon were behaving in an issue-
conscious or even rational manner.

Up to this point the respondents were being asked
their personal policy preferences. Now the authors
asked respondents what they perceived were
Nixon's or McGovern's policy positions on several
important issues. The measuring device was a sev-
en-point scale on which the candidate's position
could be marked. McGovern was perceived as far to
the left on all issues, and Nixon appeared closer to
the position of the majority of the electorate. The authors now compute what they call the "expected
normal vote," a concept based on an erudite analysis
of the trends in party identification. This analysis
presumably brings out long-term trends only; thus,
variations from the "expected normal vote" are by

definition short-term trends associated with a particular election. It turned out that McGovern was well below the expected normal vote in almost all categories.

Ultimately the authors use a highly sophisticated statistical procedure to account for the relative importance of issues in determining the vote as compared to party identification. The associates of the same organization that gave us *The American Voter* conclude: ". . . As an explanation of the vote in 1972 issues were at least equally important as party identification."[9] Or in simpler English, the voters knew more than they did twenty years ago about political issues and how parties stand on them, and they vote accordingly.

Some of the writers quoted here have not only stressed the development of voter consciousness on specific issues but have suggested also the growth of a set of consistent attitudes or even an ideology. Let us conclude our survey with one writer who also sees some attitude development. As suggested earlier, a voter would display attitude consistency if he favored Medicare, public housing, and Old Age Assistance because all three programs vest in government the responsibility for a variety of economic matters traditionally left to the individual. Studies following up on *The American Voter,* one by Converse[10] and another by Key,[11] found a complete lack of consistency. The general explanation was that the mass public had neither the educational background nor the intellectual capacity to deal with the

abstract concepts that sustain an organized and
consistent set of beliefs over a wide range of political
issues. More recently Norman Nie has produced a
study entitled "Mass Belief Systems Revisited:
Political Change and Attitude Structure." It appears in the August, 1974 issue of the *Journal of
Politics*.[12] Nie's argument is that within relatively
recent years Americans have on a number of issues
developed consistent mass belief systems. Nie's examination of Survey Research Center data con-
vinces him that politics is no longer perceived as a
buzzing confusion of separate and unrelated issues.
The five issue-areas for which he has comparable
data may be described as social welfare, welfare
measures specific for blacks, the size of government,
racial integration in the schools, and the cold war.
Nie found that for 1964 there was a dramatic
change in the levels of attitude consistency. The
degree of association between attitudes on each of
the five issues had increased, and in almost all cases
the increases are quite substantial. The pattern for
1972 is a little more complex. Yet it turns out that
all relationships not involving the size of government have maintained themselves or increased.
Correlations among all issue-areas, both foreign
and domestic, with the exception of the size of government are above .25 in 1972.

Ideological consistency may be discussed under
three categories, namely, overall index of consistency, attitude of domestic consistency, and consistency between domestic and foreign issues. In all

three categories there occurred an impressive growth in consistency between 1960 and 1964, and this change held with only trifling variation through 1968, 1971, and 1972. Thus voters increased their consistency relative to domestic issues, to foreign policy issues, and in their consistency between domestic and foreign issues. The last increase in consistency is of interest because it indicates that foreign policy attitudes, at least as measured by positions on the cold war, have increasingly become part of the public's general stance on the issues. Before one can conclude that we have developed a mass belief system approximating an ideology, there is the question as to how many different kinds of issues and over how wide a scope of subject matter they must range. One datum often cited as absence of any generalized liberal/conservative ideology has been the lack of any relationship between positions such as welfare, race, and foreign policy on the one hand and attitudes toward civil liberties on the other. Nie finds an impressive relationship between attitudes toward amnesty on the one hand and welfare, black welfare, integration, and the cold war on the other.

Finally it may be useful to compare these instances of attitude consistency with those of candidates for Congress in 1958 as measured by Converse. He found that the congressional candidates did, indeed, have a higher level of consistency than the voters, but by 1964 the mass of voters exceeded the 1958 candidates' degree of consistency and has remained ahead of it ever since. This higher consistency was especially true of attitudes on domestic issues.

So we must now approach the question of why the greater level of attitudinal consistency. A reasonable hunch might be the impressive increase in the median level of education since 1956. Yet Nie shoots down this hypothesis by comparing the growth of attitudinal consistency of a group of college graduates with a sample of high-school dropouts. He finds about the same degree of increase in consistency between 1956 and 1972 for both groups. Let us recall that Pomper[13] reached the same conclusion concerning education. A second hypothesis is the increased salience of politics, that is, more crisis politics, and this has made people regard politics as more central to their lives. To test this hypothesis, Nie must demonstrate that the level of salience of politics has increased, and, secondly, that consistency has increased primarily among those to whom politics has become more salient. Nie begins by showing the changing levels of attitude consistency through time for two levels of interest—those very interested in politics and those not interested at all. Oddly enough, it is the disinterested that have increased their consistency slightly. At this point Nie hypothesizes that the disinterested may fall into two classes: the disenchanted and the quiescent. The former profess to be disinterested because they now distrust their government and are alienated. The quiescent are truly uninterested but still trust their government. To test this hypothesis, Nie makes use of a battery of questions on cynicism toward governmental processes from 1964 onward. He finds that the proportion of "uninterested" citizens who respond to these questions in a predominately disenchanted manner has grown steadily since 1964. In 1964 and 1968, only the interested citizens who were "positively involved" were characterized by high levels of consistency. ("Positively involved" means both interested in politics and having a reasonably optimistic view of the nation's future.) In 1972, this group was still consistent. But in 1972, there is a sharp increase in a second group that has ideological consistency but that professes no interest in government. This group, which is nearly as large as the interested group, was apparently a group that had earlier registered considerable interest but had run out of faith and optimism in the ability of their government to cope with the problems of the era. While professing disinterest, they nonetheless held a consistent set of views. Their cynicism does not mean that they regard politics as having little effect on their lives; rather their loss of faith has caused many people to withdraw from politics in frustration.

At the risk of repeating the obvious, let us point out how this argument differs from the long-accepted theory that mass beliefs are associated with enduring characteristics of the mass public. The absence of consistency was explained in terms of the public's intellectual inability to put together a consistent point of view. Yet let us recall that the earlier data came from the year 1956, the middle of the Eisenhower era. Politics was perceived at that time as a relaxing sideshow. Yet by the middle and late 1960s, Americans witnessed one political crisis after another: urban rioting, increased militancy within the civil-rights movement, political assassinations, and ever-deeper involvement in the quagmire of the Vietnamese War. The argument presented here is that the public has now come to perceive politics as more salient—more important and vital to their daily lives. Of course, the feeling of the increased relevance of politics experienced in the middle and late 1960s may not continue. Instead, there may be a return to the torpor of the earlier era. However, even if this should occur, it would still dispel the theory that attitude inconsistency is based on intellectual inadequacy and built-in indifference to politics.

There is a considerable difference between discovering a relationship between attitudinal consistency and demonstrating that it has an impact on political behavior. Nie demonstrates this impact in a table reproduced below revealing that a correlation between liberal/conservative attitudes and presidential vote choice (Democratic or Republican) 1956–1972, produces the now familiar pattern. Related to the vote choice are all domestic issues, the average for all issue-areas, average for attitudes on the cold war, and the average for civil liberties attitudes. In 1956 and 1960 the relationship between attitudes and vote was low. In 1964 three of these four statistics took a dramatic spurt upward. They faltered briefly in 1968, but in 1972 all four measurements of attitude showed a high correlation with the presidential vote choice.

TABLE 1
Comparison of Correlations
(Gammas) with Attitudes 1956–72[a]

	1956	1960	1964	1968	1972
Presidential voting and attitudes	.16	.21	.57	.43	.53
Party identification and attitudes	.12	.15	.32	.26	.16
Difference	.04	.06	.25	.17	.37

[a]Nie, p. 586.

The foregoing suggests the possibility of a party realignment. As Nie puts it:[14]

At the beginning of the period under investigation, political attitudes had little relationship to either presidential voting or partisan identification. As we have shown, the relationship between attitudes and presidential voting has risen dramatically from the pre- to the post-1964 period. The relationship between these attitudes and the more permanent party allegiance has undergone a more complex pattern of change. In 1956 attitudes on

political issues bore little or no relationship to party
identification. In 1964 and to a lesser degree in
1968, this picture appeared to have changed somewhat: while rising less rapidly and dramatically
than the relationship between attitudes and presidential voting, that between attitudes and party
allegiance had increased substantially over the
1956 level. As Pomper argues, in 1964 and 1968 it
appeared that the parties were .... effecting a
realignment which reinforced existing party divisions: a liberal Democratic party and a conservative Republican one. In 1972, however, while attitude consistency in the mass public remained at
the same high level as in 1968 and the impact of
attitudes on the vote had increased somewhat, the
parties in 1972 no longer appeared to be reflecting
attitudes which are increasingly aligned on a left-
right continuum. In fact, the average gamma falls
almost to the 1956 level. This drop raises the spectre
of a very different kind of realignment ... , one in
which new partisan attachments may form that are
not based on an increasingly liberal Democratic
party versus an increasingly conservative Republican party.

The question of realignment will be the subject of
the following three chapters. The second and fourth
will deal with the question whether parties will
realign along the "logical" liberal/conservative
basis or whether the reshuffling will be along the
different line suggested above. The third chapter
will speculate on how the South will fit into the
picture.

Two

ARE AMERICAN PARTIES

FACING REALIGNMENT

OR DISINTEGRATION?

The late V. O. Key fathered the idea of the critical election, defining it as one in which the realignment of voters was both sharp and durable. Yet Key left a large number of unanswered questions. For instance, he discovered critical elections by looking backward into history, but he offered us few clues for predicting the future. In any presidential election the realignment might be sharp, but the only way to tell whether or not it was durable would be to wait patiently through the next couple of elections.

However, Key did drive home one all-important
idea: some elections are more important than others. In few presidential elections does each party
have a 50–50 chance. After a critical election, the
winning party establishes itself as the normal
majority party for a number of elections to come—
for an entire era. Key based his arguments on actual
election returns rather than on the then-emerging
concept of party identification, and he wrote at a
time when it was normal for the same party to
control both Congress and the Presidency.

Not all subsequent writers can agree on the exact
date of a realignment. Key argued originally for
1928 as the realigning year. Later writers have
talked about a realigning era. The change does not
come about in one election; there may be a series of
preliminary shocks rather than one grand earth-
quake. And there may be minor sectional realignments which do not have any immediate effect on
the entire nation. Key's idea has spawned a small
industry of writing on party realignment. But the
interest in the subject is timely. The last era—the
era of the New Deal coalition—has lasted a long
time. Judged by the average length of such eras—28
years—a realignment is long overdue. The issues
that created this alignment have faded and dulled
with the passage of time. Finally, a mountain of
evidence attests to an increase in ticket-splitting as
well as the practice of voters identifying themselves
as Independents.

One of the most stimulating writers on realignment theory is James L. Sundquist, author of *The Dynamics of the Party System*.[1] Sundquist sets forth a series of hypotheses as to the conditions that he has found to be associated with realignment as he has traced the history of American parties. The first requirement is the introduction of a new political issue which must be translatable into a political question. It is not enough to say, for instance, that there occurred an Industrial Revolution. The three major realignments of our history involved political questions. The first was what should the government do about slavery? The second was what should the government do about the hardships of the farmers and about inequality in the distribution of wealth and income among regions and classes? The third was what should the government do about the Great Depression?

To bring about a realignment, the new issue must cut across the existing lines of party cleavage. If the parties have been split on an economic or regional basis, the introduction of a moral issue would cut across the existing lines of cleavage. Slavery is the obvious example that comes to mind. Naturally the crosscutting idea must be a powerful one—powerful enough to dominate all political debate and eventually polarize the nation. Political positions become moral absolutes, and compromise becomes impossible.

Also the realigning issue must be one on which major political groups take not only distinct and opposing policy positions but positions that are easily dramatized and understood. Technical and abstract questions incomprehensible to the average voter will not generate the passion necessary to produce a realignment. The power and polarizing effect of the new issue will be greater if some of the emotional force of the older issues has faded with time.

The normal response of a major party is to try to straddle the new issue. A difficulty with this response is that there are always groups within each party more concerned with victory for their issue than with electoral success. These groups which, in effect, would rather be right than President, form at each pole of the opinion spectrum. At one pole are the champions of the new issue; at the other pole are its most intense opponents. Now is the time that the centrist politicians emerge and get to work. Emotional and economic ties make most voters unwilling to see their party disrupted, and the centrists, who are often in positions of the greatest authority, have a stake in keeping the party together. Incidentally the polar forces can form more rapidly and effectively if the party out of power is the one with the greater predisposition toward the new issue. The party in power is in a position to use patronage and all other weapons and authority at its disposal to keep the majority of its important figures in line.

The out party, on the other hand, is often in an entirely different position. It is likely to be in the midst of a more or less bitter struggle for leadership since there will be no established position of leadership. Some leader aspiring for the presidential nomination may seize upon the new and divisive issue and exploit it fully, often in a thoroughly irresponsible fashion.

A realignment crisis is precipitated when the moderate centrist politicians lose control of one or both of the major parties—that is, of policy and nominations—to one or the other of the polar forces. In the instances involving Presidents Cleveland and Hoover, neither of whom fit the normal pattern of a party politician, these men themselves became the leaders of one of the polar forces. Once this occurred, the realignment crisis was precipitated.

Realignment reaches its climax in one or more critical elections that center on the realigning issue and resolve it, but the process may extend over a considerable period both before and after the critical election. Moreover, realignment may involve the destruction of one of the old parties and its replacement by a new one. Of course, if new issues arise that coincide with the existing line of party cleavage, they increase the distance between the parties and reinforce the existing alignment.

So much for theory. Let us return to the current situation. The New Deal is history, yet no basic realignment has occurred since the one which inaugurated that era, although there have been real possibilities of such a development. In fact, since the New Deal era, there have been four crosscutting issues that contained the potentialities of a realignment. The first, in the late 1940s and early

1950s, was Communism. The second, which developed in the 1950s, was race. The third, in the 1960s, was Vietnam. The fourth, equally recent, was "Law and Order," which came to be combined with aspects of race and Vietnam.

At the end of the war, "the Iron Curtain fell across Europe, and millions of Eastern Europeans with millions of relatives in America found communism imposed upon them, all seemingly with the acquiescence of Roosevelt at Yalta."[2] The Russians supported powerful internal communist threats to the governments of Italy, Greece, France, and other countries. At first most of the leaders of the Republican party straddled the issue because many of them had supported Roosevelt's wartime policies and believed in them. McCarthy, an obscure senator, had nothing to lose by exploiting the issue. His charges may have had some small but immeasurable effect on the size of the Eisenhower victory in 1952. But a polar leader is eventually driven to attack even the centrist leaders of his own party if he is to acquire and retain prominence. What McCarthy needed was some anti-communism measure that could be made to appear of great significance to the country but that would so offend substantial elements within the Democratic party that they would be driven to the same pole as the domestic Communists. McCarthy and associates could come up with no such issue, and soon the centrist Democrats, including such figures as Senator Hubert Humphrey, were competing with the Republicans to sponsor measures of domestic communist control. McCarthy eventually weakened his case by too vigorous an attack on the leaders of his own party.

Race was another potentially realigning issue, and, of course, its potentialities are not dead. During the 1948 Democratic National Convention, the centrists temporarily lost control of the party, and the liberals wrote into the platform a stronger civil rights plank than had been contemplated by the Platform Committee. The result was the formation of the States' Rights party and the loss of four Deep South states and their 39 electoral votes in 1948. This lesson was not lost upon the Democrats at the time of the next convention. Their nominee was Adlai Stevenson, who up to that time had not taken a strong pro-civil rights position. Selected as his running mate was Alabama's Senator John Sparkman, a long-time economic liberal. Stevenson was renominated in 1956 along with Tennessee's Estes Kefauver. In both conventions the platform position on civil rights was a difficult and challenging one for the Democratic centrist leadership to handle, but they dealt with it in such a fashion that it was not a direct cause of the loss of any electoral votes. It will be stressed at a later time that it was not states of the Deep South that defected to the Republicans in 1952 and 1956, and a nonracial interpretation will be argued.

In 1960 the Democratic convention wrote a strong civil rights plank, but President Kennedy tried to steer a centrist course and to conciliate the powerful southern congressmen with whom he had to work in Congress. Actually it was his successor, Lyndon Johnson, the first southern President in a century, who moved away from the center and assumed the leadership in securing the enactment of the Civil Rights Act of 1964 and the Voting Rights Act of 1965 with substantial Republican support in Congress on both pieces of legislation. Although Senator Goldwater adopted an urbane segregationist stand in his 1964 campaign, the Republican party nationally has shown no sign of realigning itself as a segregationist organization. Both integrationist and segregationist extremists exist in the party, but it seems generally under the control of a centrist group. Thus the drastic bits of legislation of 1964 and 1965 taken under Johnson's leadership fizzled as realigning possibilities.

But now the racial issue ceased to be merely a southern problem, and racial conflict in one form or another appeared in all sections of the country. So it was that by the time the crisis precipitated by the racial issue was well advanced it had become intertwined with an issue sometimes known as "law and order," and the domestic controversy over Vietnam had risen to its height. Both of these matters had their impact on the still explosive racial issue.

The growth of domestic resistance to the Vietnamese war is too long and complex to be recounted here. Suffice it to say that a vocal minority, centered in the young people who would have to fight the war, proved to have an effective veto on this item of foreign policy and eventually compelled the retirement of a President and the redirection of American foreign policy. The polar forces mobilizing against the war in Vietnam grew in strength and entered the political arena under the leadership of Senator Eugene McCarthy. As soon as it appeared that opposition to the war was a popular and viable issue, Robert Kennedy rushed to the head of the polar forces and demanded that the Asian policy be reversed. The centrist forces now reappeared. President Johnson first called a halt to the bombing of North Vietnam, then entered into peace negotiations. Moreover, he announced his plans not to run for re-election. Senator Humphrey, the Democratic nominee in 1968, promised to do his best to negotiate a settlement. Nixon, perceived as more of a hawk than Humphrey, claimed to have a plan for peace. Third party candidate George Wallace alone clung to the hawkish position. It turned out that the two major parties both yielded to the basic demands of the peace advocates that the American policy be reversed, and they yielded at about the same time. Thus, in the end a realignment of the party system on Vietnam was averted.

Between 1966 and 1969 there arose a number of separate problems which were nonetheless merged in the popular mind under the caption of the "social issue" or "law and order." Crime was clearly on the increase. Although many people regarded crime as having nothing to do with race, the most terrifying breakdown in law and order was the eruption of widespread rioting in the black ghettos in almost every major city in the country and in many minor ones. So when some whites talked about "law and order," they meant keeping black crime and disorder out of white neighborhoods. Law and order as an idea had racial overtones to many Americans; to others it did not.

Law-and-order was related to the Vietnamese issue because it precipitated disrespect for law in the form of burning of the flag and of draft cards, ransacking of draft offices, interference with military and industrial recruitment on campuses, harassment of defense research and ROTC organizations, and demonstrations that frequently got out of control.

Many university students were not only alienated by the war but disaffected generally. They adopted new hair styles and music and experimented with newer and seemingly more dangerous drugs. Campus riots occurred over both Vietnam and a range of other grievances. Old standards of sexual morality seemed everywhere to be disintegrating. Pornography came out from under the counter, increased one hundred-fold in volume, and now appeared openly in the display cases.

In the public perception, all these things merged. Ghetto riots, campus riots, street crime, anti-Vietnam marches, poor peoples' marches, drugs, pornography, welfarism, rising taxes, all had a common thread: the breakdown of family and social discipline, of order, of concepts of duty, of respect for law, of public and private morality.[3]

The "social issue" resulted in get-tough advocates being elected mayor in a number of cities. Vice-President Agnew endeavored to blame the increase in crime and social ills on the Democrats. Yet to turn the social issue into a polarizing one that would realign voters in their favor, the Republicans would have to maneuver the Democrats to the point where that party would be perceived as pro-crime and pro-violence. A few leading Democrats took the bait with remarks to the effect that if they had lived under conditions endured by ghetto dwellers they might have become riot leaders themselves. However, the Democratic centrist majority was not so inept. Soon both parties were vying with one another in advancing proposals to do something about these various social evils. The prudent reaction of the Democrats kept all this from being a realigning issue. Yet, this is not the same thing as saying that the social issue, like race, may not provide the basis for party alignment at some time in the future.

So the most menacing issues that threatened realignment in the mid-1970s have produced no such realignment. But another change in the voter's relationship to his party may have occurred. Much evidence suggests that voters are now less firmly attached to their party. Modern students would have to have explained to them the expression "yellow dog Democrat." One evidence of this decreased attachment is the rise of ticket-splitting. Voters support the nominee of one party for president and the nominees of the other party for governor, senator, or congressman. Even when a president wins by a landslide, one of three congressional districts is carried by a congressman of a different party than the one who swept the district for the presidency. A comparable analysis of split outcomes in gubernatorial and senatorial elections between 1914 and 1970 shows the same trend. From 1962 through 1970 more than 44% of the states electing both a governor and a senator split their choices between the parties. Only once in the 24 election years from 1914 to 1960 had the proportion exceeded 28%.[4] Even the Survey Research Center, which originated the idea of strong or weak identifiers to describe the voter's relationship to his party, played down party identification as a factor in the 1972 election.

Parallel with all this, the poll takers are finding an increase in the number of voters who classify themselves as Independents rather than as Republicans or Democrats. In the 1950s the number of self-avowed Independents was relatively small, hovering somewhere around 10%, or, if we include those leaning toward one party or the other, 22%. Now both Gallup and the Survey Research Center agree that the Independents are more numerous than the Republicans. The Survey Research people, who put the Independent figure at 31% in 1970, would pinpoint the date of change somewhere in 1965. In their gross shifts the Republicans have suffered a loss of 5 percentage points, the Democrats a loss of 2 percentage points, whereas the Independents have gained 8 percentage points. These changes are not uniform among all demographic groups of the nation, a matter which will be discussed at a later time.

Yet all the foregoing discussion ignores the fact that parties may be disintegrating rather than realigning. The term *disintegrating* is not the precise word needed here because it implies a patterning of political competition in which we would have in fact nationwide nonpartisan elections. *Nonpartisanship* must be regarded as a relative rather than an absolute term. To have complete nonpartisanship one would have to rank the country at the zero end of some scale of partisan feeling, and no part of the foregoing evidence would justify this conclusion. Of course, one might argue that this was akin to the strategy of the Committee to Re-elect the President. Here, practically all available cash was channeled through this organization, and every Republican congressman was left to finance his own campaign.

What we are really talking about here is not the disintegration of parties but the lessening of their influence. Further, we are dealing with both long-term and short-term reasons for this decline. Consider the development of civil service systems at state and local levels in the last fifty years. The decline in patronage means the weakening of party muscle. Moreover, newspapers nowadays rarely endorse straight-ticket voting, and an organization such as the League of Women Voters would look askance at the mere suggestion of a straight-ticket vote.

However, these long-term forces cannot be treated as the causes of split-ticket voting or the increasing number of Independents. Since these two developments date only to the troubled 1960s, they could be explained by such short-term developments as white southerners unhappy about race and Catholics unhappy about the social issue. Both groups have produced an increasing number of Independents. Another short-term explanation is the demonstrated policy differences between the Democrats supporting McGovern and the Democrats defecting to Nixon. Here the policy differences were not on one overriding issue, and most of these voters were unwilling to vote a straight Republican ticket. They merely scratched the head of the ticket and cast a split ballot.

Race is still a very possible realigning issue. One can think of this in connection with either pole—the activities of the Wallace movement or a possible black revolt from the Democratic party. Yet Wallace supporters showed no tendency to identify with the Republicans, that is, the 1968 Wallace supporters did not adopt a Republican identification in 1972. Moreover, at least in the South in 1968, Wallace and Nixon support came from entirely different socioeconomic strata. Although for a time it appeared that Governor Wallace might be a kingmaker at the 1976 Democratic Convention, his own nomination was never likely.

A more dangerous development would be for American blacks to leave the Democratic party and seek an identity in an all-black party. This eventuality might very well frighten large numbers of white Democrats into either a revived Republican party or an entirely new conservative party. An all black party would imply that black leaders are more interested in "soul" and a quest for identity than in political reality. With 15 blacks in the U.S. House under the Democratic banner and an ever-increasing number in lesser posts throughout the nation in the same party, we find an increasing number of blacks who have a personal and power stake in the success of the Democratic party. They occupy positions of power, respect, and influence. Should they abandon the party, they would find themselves an isolated and powerless pressure group.

Yet none of the foregoing lays to rest the possibility of a realignment of parties. Surely the growth of ticket-splitting and the increasing number of Independents do not suggest either health or stability of the present alignment any more than does the fact that only 58% of Democratic identifiers supported McGovern. Race as an issue in the form of legal segregation in the South is dead, but race in a different form is now a national issue and one not successfully straddled. The Democrats have adjusted to the social issue by electing some tough cops for mayors, but this has not settled the question. It has many facets, and its meaning is ever-changing. Realignment is still within the realm of possibility, and we cannot avoid addressing ourselves to this issue.

In commenting about realignment, we should consider three possible options. First, there could be a basic realignment along "logical" economic lines. This would put all Republican economic liberals into the Democratic party and all economically conservative Democrats into the Republican party: Javits to the Democrats, Eastland to the Republicans. Secondly, there could be no basic change, no realignment. Instead we could continue with the considerably battered outline of the New Deal coalition with minimal increase in its class basis if the recession continues for a long time. If anyone feels that the coalition has outlived its origins and is therefore illogical, let us recall the Appalachian Republicans whose party loyalty has outlived its origins by over a century. Thirdly, one might contemplate a basic realignment but in a different direction.

The first alternative, a liberal/conservative realignment assumes that the issues that created the New Deal realignment will be reenforced and the party system converted to one based on "logical" economic clashes. Certain of the studies discussed in the preceding chapter, particularly Pomper's studies, suggest this possibility. He demonstrated through 1968 an increased relation between party identification and issue preferences, an increased perception of party differences, and a greater agreement on which party is the more liberal. Yet of the six questions he used, five dealt with economic issues. In contrast, the SRC's study of the 1972 election and the piece by Nie introduce questions about amnesty, campus unrest, urban riots, legalization of marijuana, abortion, and the rights of women. Here we have a different set of issues— issues that crosscut the economic ones of the New Deal alignment. For 1972 both Nie and the SRC found an impressive correlation between the position of the voter on issues and his vote for President, yet both found little relationship between party identification and issue stand. So an analysis of the 1972 election gives little comfort to the idea of a neat liberal/conservative realignment. Nor does the growth of ticket-splitting and the increasing number of Independents. If Republicans were emerging as the conservative party, they should have produced a gain in congressional strength in 1970 as was true of the Democrats in 1934, and certainly Nixon should have brought in a controlling majority on the basis of his landslide in 1972. Yet one cannot afford to dismiss this liberal/ conservative development entirely; in fact, it will be employed to explain the rise of the Southern Republicans. Finally, since any discussion of realignment must deal with the crosscutting issues of race and the social issue, we shall consider in Chapter 4 the possibility of an alignment based on a set of noneconomic issues.

Three

THE ROLE OF THE SOUTH

IN A REALIGNMENT

Anyone who has read presidential election returns in the last couple of decades is aware of the tremendous growth in presidential Republicanism in the South. Students have to be reminded that there was once such a thing as the Solid South the way they have to be taught that California once belonged to Mexico. They were not around to experience either of the earlier two eras. The change in southern voting behavior is the best example of realignment that the nation has to offer. Yet even a profound regional realignment is obviously not a national one.

In a purely passive sense the South may have been responsible for initiating race as one of the two realigning factors that may cause the final demise of the New Deal coalition. Eventually there came a time outside the South when the ethnic and labor beneficiaries of the New Deal came to be threatened by its black beneficiaries. But we must not place too direct an emphasis on race. The change has been due to two separate factors—economics and race— with race generally the intervening variable.

The story begins with a now forgotten character, Republican Congressman Oscar DePriest. Many people are aware that Alabama has a black belt, a band of fertile black soil stretching across the south central section of the state. But Chicago also has a black belt, which produces neither cotton nor cattle, but which as early as 1928 housed an impressively larger number of blacks. The great northward migration of blacks began around 1910. In 1920 the census takers found that 19 percent of the nation's blacks lived outside the South, and by 1930 that figure had risen to 26 percent.[1] Thus it came to pass that on the day in 1928 when Herbert Hoover was elected President there was elected from Chicago's black belt a fellow Republican. He was Congressman Oscar DePriest, the first black in Congress since the year 1901.

It is well to recall that Franklin Roosevelt did practically nothing for blacks as such. During the first year of World War II, after being subjected to considerable pressure, he finally issued on presidential authority a wartime FEPC. The great benefits to blacks from the New Deal were spinoffs from other policies. Probably the most important example was the assumption by the federal government of a large-scale policy of direct relief. Direct relief went to all persons in desperate need. What group in the population had a higher percentage of unemployed and persons in desperate need than the blacks? There followed what must surely be adjudged a case of rational political behavior. Blacks, being reasonable men, perceived that it did indeed make a difference which party was in power in Washington. So when DePriest ran for re-election in 1934, he was defeated by a black Democrat, and the party that elected over one hundred white-supremacist congressmen from the South now acquired a black colleague.

Not all political observers focused their attention on this 1934 development or put a reasonable interpretation on it. Such persons were surprised to learn that in the 1936 landslide for Roosevelt approximately 75 percent of all American blacks voted Democratic and rejected the party of Lincoln. Of course, other factors may have contributed to the shift. Mrs. Roosevelt went out of her way to be courteous to blacks, and newspaper photographs of her with black groups or being helped out of a car by a black ROTC cadet were commonplace. The Democratic administration awakened belatedly to its op-

portunities. Having had long experience working
with non-WASP groups, it knew the importance of
passing out various middle-level jobs, and all of
these were duly publicized in the black press. Cynics
may offer yet another reason, which may have considerable validity. By 1936 Democratic mayors had
replaced Republicans in most of the nation's major
cities. If one is running a numbers game or one of the
other rackets that reportedly flourished more
widely in the ghetto than in the white-collar suburbs, it is prudent to adopt the same political faith
as the mayor and the chief of police.

The northward migration of blacks continued
even throughout the Depression decade, a time
when white southerners were returning home from
Detroit. The 1940 census reported 28% of American
blacks living outside the South. World War II was,
of course, the great stimulus for black migration
from the South, and by 1950, 37.5% of the black
population lived outside the southern region.
Blacks had been loyal Democrats in 1940 and again
in 1944. An elementary rule of politics is that one
must provide some satisfactions—either material or
psychological—to one's loyal supporters. In early
1948 President Harry Truman, who had learned as
a senator from Missouri the vital importance of
support by Democratic blacks in Kansas City, presented to Congress a civil rights program, five
points of which dealt with proposals to improve the
status of blacks. The proposal never got out of congressional committee, but it did reappear dramati-

cally in the news at the time of the Democratic convention. Centrist leaders of the party came out of the platform committee with some modified and more restricted proposals. A floor fight emerged when Texan Dan Moody urged that the provisions be further weakened. This produced a fracas in which the then mayor of Minneapolis, Hubert Humphrey, was able to carry the day for a set of proposals rather more far-reaching than the platform committee or the President wanted.

As the band played Dixie, the entire Mississippi delegation and half of the Alabama delegation (not including youthful George C. Wallace) marched out of the convention hall. These delegates formed the nucleus of an informal convention that met shortly in Birmingham to create the States' Rights party. It was in fact purely a white supremacy party; it had no general interest in making states more active and vital units of government. The term meant merely the "right" of the white majority of any state to retain the pattern of white supremacy. The States' Righters secured the electoral vote of the four states in which Thurmond was the official Democratic nominee. These states were Mississippi, Alabama, South Carolina, and Louisiana. Truman carried the other seven states of the South along with an even 50% of the popular vote. Dewey carried no states but secured 26.8% of the popular vote to Thurmond's 22.6%. The Dixiecrats won only in a region within a region.

Although race was potentially a party-splitting

issue, there were some odd crosscurrents within the
Democratic party. The party could offer segregationist southern white farmers subsidies for not
growing too much tobacco while at the same time
pledging themselves to take the Fourteenth and
Fifteenth Amendments more seriously.

Although Thurmond failed in his effort to throw
the contest into the Electoral College, the election of
1948 did have an impact. As one Birmingham
newspaper commentator put it, "When the Democratic party ceases to be the party of white supremacy, the deepest basis of Democratic loyalty has
been destroyed." The Democrats had proved themselves no longer trustworthy on the racial issue.
Now a kind of southern liberation took place.
Southern whites, now no longer in bondage to the
party of white supremacy, were free to vote their
economic convictions.

It is these economic changes that deserve the
greatest emphasis. No one needs to be reminded
that the South was the economically underdeveloped section of the nation, and it was World War
II that gave the region a tremendous shove toward
industrialization. And this drive toward industrialization increased in momentum throughout the
post-war years. Although it was the 1952 election
that was to show the real impact of the new prosperity on newly prosperous southerners, there had
been earlier indications that business-oriented
southerners had Republican sympathies. Back in
1928 the general finding was that there was an

inverse relationship between a county's Negro
population and the size of the Republican vote.
However, even with the black population held constant, there was an excessive amount of Republicanism in the area's few large cities. By 1948 Republican strength in such Texas metropolitan
centers as Houston and Dallas was truly impressive. A partial explanation of Republican success in
1952 and 1956 was the personality of Dwight
Eisenhower. Obviously the Republicans had acquired a candidate with real charisma. Yet it would
be inexcusably shallow to attribute the Republican
successes to the popularity of Eisenhower. Were this
true, his percentage would have been relatively uniform among all the one thousand-odd counties of the
South. Such was not the case. In the first place, he
won the electoral votes of four states in the rim
South—Virginia, Tennessee, Florida, and Texas.
Elsewhere in the region, particularly in the Deep
South, his showing was unimpressive (except in
1956 when he carried Louisiana due to the development of a segregationist third party there).
Throughout all areas of the South his greatest
strength was in the metropolitan areas. This was
true both in an absolute sense and in the sense of
percentage-point gain over previous presidential
elections. Within these metropolitan areas his support was strongest in the wards and precincts where
the average home value and median rental were the
highest. He carried the most prosperous neighborhoods of large southern cities often by absurdly lop-

sided proportions. The whole effect suggested a
rerun of the 1936 election in the North when upper-
income groups first expressed their repudiation of
the New Deal. In 1960 Nixon carried three of the
southern rim states—Virginia, Florida, and Tennessee. His percentage of the total southern vote—
46%—was only three percentage-points below
Eisenhower's best in 1956.

The theory of party realignment has not developed to the point where anyone can say firmly
that it always begins at the presidential level and
moves down. In any event this is precisely what has
happened in the South. Not until after Nixon's defeat in 1960 was much real attention given to lesser
offices. As indicated in another connection, about
one-third of the South's seats in the House of Representatives (34 of 108) were in the hands of the Republican party by 1972. More important, the party
made a practice of contesting more and more seats
instead of yielding them up as hopeless and eventually grasped the peculiar importance of contesting
an election when a Democratic incumbent of long
standing voluntarily leaves the scene. Republicans
had occupied (or still occupy) the executive man-
sions of Arkansas, Florida, Virginia, Tennessee,
North Carolina, and South Carolina. Tennessee,
Florida, North Carolina, South Carolina, Virginia,
and Texas have elected Republican senators. Below
them are a host of lesser GOP officials.

The presidential election of 1964 was an aberra-
tion so far as any southern realignment is con-

cerned. Goldwater's vote against the Civil Rights
Act of 1964 suddenly converted him into the white
man's candidate. He carried the five states of the
Deep South and lost the other six, five of which had
been carried by Eisenhower in 1956. The election is
not in harmony with the pattern of Republican
gains from 1952 through 1960 when it appeared
that the gains were being made on economic issues.

The presidential election of 1968 showed two con-
tradictory facts about possible realignment. First, it
showed that only a very small percentage of southerners held the Democratic party in high esteem.
Only Texas gave the party its electoral votes. Secondly, George Wallace carried five states—
Louisiana, Mississippi, Alabama, Georgia, and Arkansas. Although the election showed that a de-
creasing number of southerners loved the Democratic party, it is hard to infer from the 1968 election
results the notion that the majority of southerners
want to be converted to Republicanism. It should be
pointed out that the southerners who voted for Wallace rather than Nixon were an entirely different
group of people. The use of factor analysis with
nineteen variables (plus the three candidates) for
each of the one thousand southern counties reveals
that the Nixon vote correlated with a high-status-
urban factor at .483; the Wallace vote related to this
factor at −.411.

The election of 1970 featured the election of racially moderate Democratic governors in Arkansas,
Florida, Georgia, and South Carolina. All four of

these men had substantial backing from both races. Under the circumstances it is difficult to argue that the Southern Democratic party is being torn apart and being destroyed by the racial issue at the state level.

Examination of the 1972 election returns offers little help to the analyst. It is a little careless to say that practically all whites in the South voted for Nixon, but that is not an entirely reckless statement. Republican representation in the House of Representatives rose from 27 to a modern high of 34. However, it dropped back to the earlier figure in 1974. Presumably Watergate had its impact here as elsewhere.

Having milked all reasonable inferences from the election returns, we can now examine the results of public opinion polling. We rely on the Survey Research Center for figures on party identification of southerners in the years 1952 through 1972 both inclusive.[2] In 1952 some 74% of white southerners classified themselves as either strong or weak Democrats. By 1972 the figure had dropped to 46%. Yet if party identification is important, little has happened to gladden the hearts of southern Republicans. In 1952, 11% of white southerners identified themselves as either strong or weak Republicans. By 1972 the figure had risen only to 19%. The big change is in the growth of persons who identified themselves as Independents, and this includes the category of Independent Democrats and Independent Republicans as well as Independents with no

modifying adjective. In 1952 these three types of
Independents contributed 11% to the southern electorate. In 1964 the figure was up to 20%. Real
growth was reported in 1968, 1970, and 1972 when
the percentages were respectively 36, 39, and 34. In
1972, 66% of all southern blacks identified themselves as Democrats, 26% as Independents, and 6%
as Republicans.

Earlier, considerable attention was given to the
out-migration of blacks from the region. Now comparable attention should be given to the in-
migration of whites. The term *in-migration* may
conjure up visions of several hundred thousand old-
sters in the southern half of Florida, bringing with
them upon retirement their arthritis and their Republicanism. Yet we must not ignore the fact that
the South, or some parts thereof, is a land of oppor-
tunity for young and healthy Yankees. Ambitious
persons of this type migrate from various areas of
the North not only to such obvious places as Houston, Dallas, Atlanta, and Memphis but also to a
great number of smaller metropolitan centers. Of
all presidential voters in 1972, white migrants, defined as people who grew up outside the South,
constituted 19% of the electorate. White natives
who grew up in the South constituted 61%; blacks,
regardless of origins, made up 20%.[3]

Thirty percent of the migrants identify themselves as either strong or weak Republicans, but
another 27% identify themselves as either strong or
weak Democrats. Of native whites over 30 years of

age, 56% are either strong or weak Democrats; natives 18–30 are only 39 per cent Democratic. Democratic strength among middle-class people, both natives and migrants, has dropped impressively. In 1952, 76% of all southern whites who identified themselves as middle class professed to be either strong or weak Democrats. In 1972, the comparable figure had fallen to 47%.[4] Since the working class as used in this table includes both whites and blacks (quite incorrectly and in a misleading fashion, in my opinion) the figures are not included here. A final interesting contrast may be made between the southern natives aged 18–30 and the more venerable southerners over 30 years of age. Of the first group, some 42 per cent put themselves into one of the three categories of Independents; in the older group, the comparable figure is only 25%. However, a nationwide Gallup poll in 1967[5] broke identifiers down by age and found that 40% of respondents 21–29 classified themselves Independents in contrast to 32% in the 30–49 year age group, and 24% of those 50 and over. In view of the nearly identical percentages for both South and nation, it would be hazardous to argue that the younger generation is the leading edge of change in the South. Also it is incautious to assume that an Independent is in the midst of a transition to Republicanism. In the absence of any data to the contrary, we might assume that he will remain an Independent indefinitely or even eventually find his way back into the Democratic party.

In this connection it may be useful to compare one aspect of the behavior of white northern and southern Independents in the elections of 1964 through 1972 both inclusive. In one category are Independent Democrats, Independents, and Independent Republicans. These groups are broken down into their voting behavior in presidential elections and elections for the House of Representatives, and they are also broken down by north versus south. The odd feature here is that southern Democrats and southern Independents were rather less prone to be loyal to the Democratic presidential nominee but when compared with their Yankee brethren were more prone to be loyal in their congressional choices. Or to make the comparison at greater length, if we compare the voting behavior for President of Independent Democrats in the north and in the south, we find that the Yankees were relatively loyal in their presidential voting in the three elections 1964–1972; whereas the self-identified Independent white Democrats of the south gave percentages like 17 and 18 percent for Humphrey and McGovern. Yet when it comes to supporting nominees for the House of Representatives we find that in three of the five elections the southern group was substantially more loyal to the Democratic nominee, and in the fourth election the southern group was only slightly behind their northern cousins.[6] These data certainly do not indicate that either Independent Democrats or Independents have much interest in voting a straight Republican ticket. Had the results turned out differently, one might have had the basis for an argument that Independence is a bridge to Republicanism. The only conclusion these data justify is that we have here a bridge over troubled waters.

Southern Republicans are much weaker as measured by numbers of party identifiers than they are in terms of victories at the polls. Note the slow rise in Republican identifiers from 11 percent in 1952 to 19 percent in 1972. It is merely a comforting semantic trick to observe that the figure has nearly doubled. It may be well to recall Nie's finding of the greater consistency in attitude and voting than in attitude and party identification.[7]

The examination of the southern electorate by public opinion polling and party identification gives a much less cheerful picture of the Republicans' future in the region. In the early years of presidential Republicanism in the region, one had the nagging doubt that the explanation was Eisenhower's personality or Kennedy's Catholicism. Now it is time to say forthrightly that realignment has taken place in the South. The change began sharply in 1952 and has been durable. In the six presidential elections 1952–1972, both inclusive, the states of Virginia, Tennessee, and Florida gave their electoral votes to the Republican nominee five out of six times. All other states went Republican one or more times during that period. To repeat what was stated earlier, Florida, North Carolina, South Carolina, Tennessee, and Virginia have had both Republican senators and governors while Arkansas has

had a GOP governor and Texas a GOP senator.
Ten states had Republican congressmen serving
in 1975. The Georgia GOP, down on its luck in 1974,
had one or two congressmen throughout 1964–
1972. The last two states to elect GOP
congressmen—Mississippi and Louisiana—now
have two each. The above constitutes a realignment
within a large and important region. To insist on a
greater change in party identification as proof of
realignment is absurd in this context. Thus, in 1972
Virginia elected seven GOPers to its ten-man House
delegation, chose a Republican senator, and supported Nixon while being governed by a Republican
elected earlier. If at that point in time the majority
of Virginians wished to retain their amateur status
as Democrats, this fact does not alter the conclusion
above. Nor have realignment theorists ever used as
a criterion the idea that realignment is not complete
until the growing party captures the majority of
local offices. The South realigned to competitive two
partyism. The fragile union of blacks and less prosperous whites that carried ten states for Carter in
1976 is not a return to the pre-1952 era.

Part of the problem of discerning a pattern and
asking or answering the question about southern
realignment is the fact that it has its two sources—
economics and race. And race is the least direct
causative factor. When the Democrats nationally
began to champion civil rights, they appeared no
better than the Republicans on that issue (the GOP
having assumed an anti-Negro stance in 1964 only)

so southern voters began to vote what they perceived to be their economic advantage. Yet not all
southerners agree on economic matters. Prior to
World War II the South could be visualized as an
underdeveloped region crushed under the heel of
Wall Street. Even Alabama produced a few figures
who asserted as much—Hugo Black, Lister Hill,
John Sparkman, and James Folsom. But the new
postwar prosperity changed the region's image for
many people. It gave a vast number of young men a
vision of business prosperity within the area. There
was nothing wrong with the economic system as far
as they were concerned; all they wanted was to get a
larger cut out of it. Going somewhat beyond our
data, we may assume that many of these young men
abandoned the Baptists, joined the Episcopalians,
and learned to play golf. Whether the business men-
tality was that of the era of President McKinley or
President Harding is somewhat debatable. In any
event, membership in neither the Episcopalians nor
the Republicans accounts for George Wallace and
his numerous following. In 1954 Wallace was the
South Alabama campaign manager for populist
James Folsom; in 1968 some 52 percent of the
South's trade union members voted for Wallace for
President, and he likewise found abundant strength
in the rural areas. His following cannot make common cause with the country-club set in any simple
and direct fashion. Southern Republicans have
found a home; Wallacites are still wandering in the
wilderness, a fact that need not detract from their
long-run importance.

After breaking with Folsom, Wallace made his reputation as the number-one racist in the South. Now that racism in different forms has become nationwide and related issues are available, Wallace demonstrated the existence of a considerable market for his views. The Republican party with its present centrist national leadership cannot attract the Wallace following in the South or elsewhere. Yet different leadership of the party or of a successor party to the Republicans might attract this following. It could not be rightist leadership in the Goldwater sense because the leadership would have to favor social security and be friendly to unions. It might even favor government programs helpful to blue-collar people in general but not to blacks in particular. However, any such change would have to be part of a nationwide reshuffling along this line, and that possibility will be examined in the following chapter.

Carter's victory in all states of the South save Virginia is not out of harmony with the above argument. Ford's defeat was nowhere a rout. Only in Carter's native Georgia did he secure as much as 67 percent of the total popular vote; in Arkansas it was 65 percent. Elsewhere the percent ranged from 48 in Virginia to 56 in South Carolina. The net loss of one Republican House seat in the South is trifling; the total fell from 28 in 1974 to 27 in 1976. Had there been a wipeout of Republican strength one might have expected a return to the seven Republican seats held in 1960 or the two held in 1950. *Time* reported that Ford carried 51 percent

of the white vote nationally;[8] John Lewis's estimate
of 55 percent of the southern white vote going for
Ford seems entirely plausible. Certainly the GOP
has not lost its strong following among southern
whites.

In a general way the earlier pattern of support for
Republican presidential and congressional nominees prevailed. The more prosperous and business-
oriented southerners continued their support. Ford
and congressional nominees did well in most of
the larger metropolitan areas, and his support
weakened in the smaller towns and rural areas.
Surely no direct relationship prevailed between the
percent urban of a particular county and the GOP
percent of the vote, yet it is suggestive that all three
of Alabama's Republican congressmen represent-
ing Birmingham, Mobile, and Montgomery—the
state's three largest cities—were reelected easily.
Only where the northern pattern of black majority
in the central cities and white flight to the suburbs
prevails as in Memphis and Atlanta does the black
Democratic congressman appear. Or in so huge a
metropolis as Houston, where the black residential
areas have their own Barbara Jordan.

Blacks were the most loyal Democrats as they had
been in several previous elections, and this time
they produced a record turnout. The real switch
from recent elections was in the increased Democratic support by lower-income and nonmetropoli-
tan whites, many of whom had doubtless been Wallace supporters. *Time* reported that "among white

Baptists, most of whom live in the South and have
been voting Republican in recent elections (some
77% voted for Nixon in 1972), Carter got more than
56% of their vote."[9] This combination on which Carter forged his victory in the South—blacks and
lower-income whites—is not one that has had a long
history of agreeable relations. Carter will have to
display great political skill to keep this combination
together and prevent a Republican comeback.

Four

So far my remarks on a possible realignment have been very much on the side of timidity. Tonight I shall argue forthrightly that the old coalition can never be put together again. Predicting a far-reaching and novel realignment is not throwing caution to the winds because as plausible an argument for it can be offered as has been offered in the more timid approach.

If one is to argue the coming of a profound shakeup, great stress must be put on the post-industrial revolution and post-industrial society. Crudely defined, this concept means that we have mastered the art of manufacturing Chevrolets and bedsprings. Now an ever-increasing part of our labor force will be devoting its time to the production of services. The remark about bedsprings and Chevrolets is not entirely precise. We will still be employing large numbers of research specialists who will advise on finding a yet wider market for these products.

And this leads us into the second major topic needing stress—the growth of the knowledge industry. An ever-increasing percentage of the population toils not, neither does it spin, at least not in the historic sense. Instead an ever higher percentage of the population is engaged in the production and distribution of new knowledge. Examples of such personnel include the faculties of colleges and universities with their vastly increased enrollment since 1960, foundations and think-tanks, persons associated with the communications industry, and an entire breed of consultants who render advice not only to bankers and insurance executives but also to persons interested in eliminating poverty. Much of the work of bureaucracies at all levels of government would fall into the knowledge industry or service category.

A nearby example suggestive of what is involved is that the University of Alabama at Birmingham is now the single largest employer in Jefferson county, having edged out Tennessee Coal and Iron.

Likewise, Vanderbilt University is the largest non-governmental employer in the county in which Nashville is located. Related to the knowledge group are people who work primarily with people, particularly those who seek to uplift the downtrodden.

Now all of this change is producing a new elite. The top persons in the several activities just enumerated pretty much constitute the new elite. This is not to suggest that various business leaders in the West and the South, particularly those in smaller communities, do not enjoy a high degree of power and prestige. Yet elsewhere the close relationship between income and voting behavior has changed. In its place there has developed a kind of limousine liberalism.

Many readers will recognize these as the ideas of Walter Dean Burnham and Kevin Phillips. This is the same Phillips who a few years back wrote *The Emerging Republican Majority*.[1] He felt that the GOP would bring about a realignment by uniting the South and the West, an idea reminiscent of William Jennings Bryan. He believed that the economic conservatism of the South and West would make them the natural breeding ground for a Republican party that would remain the majority party for years to come. Phillips was close to the White House, yet he was unable to get Nixon to buy these ideas. Perhaps he could not get past Haldeman. His second volume, *Mediacracy*,[2] suggests a more chastened Phillips. He does not abandon his political geography complete but rather presents it with more sophistication and with the addition of new elements. His frequent quotations from political scientists make this less of a partisan tract.

There are those who argue that the media—especially television and its New York-based network programs—have a distinctly liberal bias. The case is made on the contention that the networks have put out an undue number of specials dealing with poverty and hunger in the United States. This whole question is tied up in the very perplexing definition of what bias is and how you distinguish it from energetic background reporting of the news. In any event, the subject matter of the relatively small number of TV specials has been in harmony with the values of the new elite.

A final basic notion is the stress on the profound and unsettling nature of the change to a post-industrial society. We may be in a political situation comparable to that of British political parties in the years 1828–1846. In those years, the parties were in a state of meaningless flux. Thereafter the parties slowly began to reorganize on principles more relevant to the times. Eventually each party developed a changed constituency and a different policy stress. All the foregoing is based on the assumption that a change to a post-industrial society is as unsettling and shattering as the change from a preindustrial society to an industrialized one.

The real change began in the mid-1960s with the Vietnamese War and the drive for the Great Soci-

ety. As will be developed later, the reactions against
the anti-Vietnamese protests were as important as
the protests themselves. But liberal leadership
failed somewhere around the period of the Great
Society. Even at the early stages a perceptive ob-
server could argue that members of the new
elite—middle-class people—were the chief beneficiaries. Money trickled down to the poverty-
stricken, but myriads of experts arose to plan the
direction of the trickle. All kinds of specialists developed an interest in the abolition of poverty. It
became what might be called in some circles a
growth industry.

It is difficult to identify an exact year of change.
Many of the central concepts of liberalism versus
conservatism are now irrelevant. In 1963 and 1964
they could be aptly applied to such issues as Medicare and Federal Aid to Education, but these questions are now moot. Medicare is here to stay, and so
are some forms of federal aid to education.

But beyond these two programs, the liberal leaders had an enormous faith in the perfectibility of
man. If only enough money were poured into care-
fully designed programs, poverty could be abolished
through the improvement of the environment and
educational opportunities of the underprivileged.
This spirit of optimism is reminiscent of the optimism that prevailed in the western world in the
first decade of this century. Here was an optimistic
belief that man could conquer all the natural obsta-
cles in his environment, a belief that persisted until

the sinking of the *Titanic*. If liberalism is thought of as increased government aid to the underprivileged, there occurs at some time a point of political diminishing returns. This point is when a governmental program designed to aid one group begins to hurt or outrage the values of some other large and powerful group. The liberal programs of the New Deal could be enacted because at that time a majority of the population was poor. Possibly one can make a distinction by noting the fact that the New Deal was both anti-elitist and somewhat individualistic. Even Social Security was dedicated to the idea of helping the individual partially compensate for the loss of income due to retirement. And Supreme Court decisions of that era sought to prevent unconstitutional discrimination against individuals, not groups. When in 1948 Ms. Sipuel[3] became the first black to enroll in the University of Oklahoma Law School, the issue ended with her enrollment. A state university could not, without violating the 14th Amendment, deny a legal education to an individual simply because she was black, yet there was no question of the University of Oklahoma having to set for itself quotas or goals as to the number of Negro law students.

In any event, war protesters as well as architects of the Great Society provoked a counter-revolution. Burnings of draft cards and flags was an activity confined to a minority of university students, and the majority of university-age people are not university students. People of all ages with

deeply instilled patriotism were infuriated. Also antagonizing was the proliferation of protest songs.
Let it be noted that both burners and singers as well
as their approving witnesses and hearers came from
middle-class or upper-middle-class families. This
was a type of elite behavior. On a cultural level
there has been a reaction against the protest songs
in the form of a tremendous growth of country-
and-western music. In 1960 there were 80 radio
stations that were full-time in the country-and-
western business. By 1970 this figure had zoomed
up to 650.

Chapter 4 called attention to the Democrats' loss
of the South. Now let us consider the falling away of
other groups. Throughout the New Deal years,
Catholics were a mainstay of the northern Democratic party. According to George Gallup, the Republican share of the Catholic vote for President
was 22% in 1960, 24% in 1964, 33% in 1968, and
53% in 1972. In New York City, the percentage was
considerably higher. "Even in Italian South
Philadelphia ... Samuel Lubell has charted the
1960–1972 GOP Presidential increment: among
131 precincts, only one backed Richard Nixon in
1960, then 12 went for Goldwater in 1964; 45 picked
Nixon in 1968; an overwhelming majority backed
Nixon in 1972."[4]

Why are Catholics and ethnics disenchanted with
the Democrats? One hypothesis is that many of
them have prospered, moved to the suburbs, and
turned Republican. This is a shaky explanation

since considerable data indicate that prospering Democrats take their party loyalty with them when they move to the suburbs. The position of the black population in the central city and the federal programs of peculiar value to blacks have been an important source of friction. The Great Society's drive for affirmative action in the hiring of blacks to compensate for past years of discrimination can be argued as morally justifiable. However, from the standpoint of the lower-income-white central city resident, he is being the victim of discrimination in reverse. A job that might very well be his is given to a black. Although the largest number of recipients of Aid to Dependent Children are white women, a much higher *percentage* of black women benefit from this program. Here again the black is perceived as a peculiar object of governmental solicitude, and the black woman is perceived as being rewarded for her "sinfulness." And white persons dwelling in neighborhoods close to the ghetto live in constant fear of its expanding into their neighborhoods and their being the victims of block-busting. Moreover, the resentment of having black Democratic mayors may very readily lead to support of Republican nominees. So the point of diminishing returns has been reached. You cannot aid one beneficiary of the New Deal coalition without antagonizing a yet larger one.

If the less fortunate whites left in the central city to compete with blacks are Catholics, there is another reason for resentment against the Democrats. The new elite leadership of the Democratic party, especially as represented by the delegates to the convention nominating McGovern, is associated with easy divorce, free love, women's liberation, and legalized abortion. These are anti-family values and incompatible with Catholic doctrine. One must stress the importance throughout U.S. history of political clashes over noneconomic values. We have experienced clashes between immigrants and early settlers. Protestant-Catholic clashes have been based on Protestant Puritanism—the notion that liquor and gambling were *per se* sinful, the Catholic position being essentially that only the abuse of these practices constitute sin. Reference to these clashes should not evoke mirth; in their day the participants were embittered and tenacious of their beliefs.

It may be misleading to stress only defection from the Democrats. The other side of the coin is what Ladd and Hadley[5] call "the inversion of the New Deal class order." They compare the votes for President, 1948–1972 and the congressional votes, 1948–1974, in terms of the socioeconomic status of the voters. In 1960 and earlier years there was an inverse relation between social status and Democratic votes. But by 1968 the relationship had disappeared for all voters and had been replaced for voters under 30 by a direct relationship. There was a similar situation when one compares the college-educated (regardless of age) with the noncollege. In the earlier years the Democrats drew a much higher percentage of support from the college-educated than from the noncollege group, but in the later period the situation was reversed in presidential voting, and in congressional voting the two groups gave the same degree of support to the Democrats.

While we are discussing causes of political division and the emergence of new elites, it might be well to note briefly the values espoused by American elites—or perhaps it is a case of elites espousing certain values and anti-elites disdaining them. The most obvious division is in the area of economic organization and forms of business wealth. From this standpoint, the Northeast (plus the Great Lakes and now the Pacific Coast) are the locale of the nation's most advanced form of economic organization. The Northeast, at least, has had this role throughout American history. It was the home of the capital needed to industrialize the underdeveloped sections, and it has the power that went with this wealth. A second difference is in the realm of culture and ideological tradition. "Hoover's best states were those with the most symphony orchestras, the highest number of library books per capita, the highest level of civic-awareness levels, the highest literacy rates, the most doctors and scientists, and the highest ratio of persons locally educated later named in *Who's Who*."[6] Using the same criteria, these areas have been Republican strongholds until very recently. But recently, and especially in 1972, the traditionally Republican elite areas were most sympathetic to the views of

McGovern. The old relationship between status and Republican voting has eroded.

A final contrast is in the area of types of religion.

> The central division is between 'pietistic' denominations and 'liturgical' denominations. Pietists are reform-minded: opposed to elaborate ceremonies, rituals ... ; in favor of ... abolition of sinful institutions. In this group [are] Congregationalists, Disciples of Christ, Quakers, Methodists, Unitarians, Presbyterians, Scandinavian Lutherans ... the Pietists demanded that the government halt the spread of slavery, overthrow the saloon and the sale of liquor.
>
> On the liturgical side were these churches: Roman Catholic, Baptists (primitive), Missouri Synod Lutheran, Episcopalian. The liturgicals emphasized ... rituals and historical doctrines. Salvation required faithful adherence to the creed, liturgy, sacraments, and hierarchy of the church .... The intrusion of government into the affairs of morality was ... a threat to the primacy of the church ... the liturgicals feared that the 'fanatical' pietists would use the government to further their moralistic crusades.[7]

Please note that the comment on Episcopalians refers to their theology, not to their median income, which would put them clearly on the elite side.

The author is ambiguous in his reference to "Baptist (primitive)." He lacks a certain feel for the South. What needs to be said is that Southwide from Texas to Virginia the Baptists are as numerous as the sands of the sea. Moreover, the classification of the Methodists among the pietists is highly questionable if one is talking about Southern Methodists, who happen to be the second largest denomination in the South. Both of these groups historically fought for the abolition of the sinful institution of the saloon. Having lost this battle, they have retained an unblemished record of a liturgical emphasis and an avoidance of involvement in social issues. Evangelist Billy Graham is the epitome of this point of view.

Now the amazing thing about the 1968 presidential convention was that it saw a simultaneous revolt by the elite and the anti-elite forces. Senator-poet Eugene McCarthy spoke for the elite in calling for immediate peace in Vietnam. George Wallace led the anti-elite in a call for military victory. Yet throughout the New Deal era and before, the elite have been the backbone of the Republican party. By 1972, they represented a large part of the strength of the Democrats.

Predictions about the future party alignment may begin with references to the internal alignment of the Republican party. Progressive Republican leaders have come from the areas of most advanced post-industrialism. These were the leaders who fought the nomination of Goldwater in 1964. These leaders as individuals are middle-class or upper-middle-class WASPs whose cultural and ideological tradition will not help them relate to the Polish-Americans or southern poor whites. So it may very well be that the GOP may be ending the time when it can be a useful vehicle for either cultural or economic conservatism. This is another way of saying that it may go the way of the Whigs.

The Democratic party may have more of the future because it is in the majority tradition. Moreover, it has more state and local officeholders. Incidentally, this begs the question whether party realignment implies a change in party identification from the President down to the sheriff. The argument advanced here hedges cautiously. However, we may call attention to the over one-quarter of the southern delegates to the U.S. House of Representatives who were elected as Republicans in 1974 and to the yet more impressive increase in Democratic strength in that body from the Northeast over a somewhat longer period of time.

Let us turn to the probable lineup of the conservative tradition, whether it goes under the Republican label or that of some new party. Racially it will be an overwhelmingly white group. Regionally, it will find great strength in the white South and in the West, at least as far west as the three Pacific Coast states. An uncritical faith in a capitalistic free economy will prevail here. Mechanized Southern Baptists, for instance, are not going to be hostile to a system that has made them three times as prosperous as their parents. There will be little that is cosmopolitan about the culture. The South in particular will contribute a strong nationalistic military posture; this results from a combination of many military bases and the region's long-standing martial tradition. Neither South nor West has shown much interest in ecology or consumerism, both post-industrial-revolution phenomena.

None of the proceeding remarks should obscure the fact that the argument sees a nationwide clash over largely noneconomic values. This coalition will be the bearers of cultural conservatism. Here the followers of George Wallace would find a natural home. Cultural conservatism includes a respect for the work ethic, opposition to pornography, what might be described as a close-the-door attitude toward sex, and the restriction of one's drug consumption to such traditional drugs as alcohol and sleeping pills. Common opposition to abortion may bring the southern Protestant fundamentalists together with Catholics and Orthodox groups of other regions. The role of women's liberation is not easy to assess, but it should be noted that several books arguing for women's traditional role have relied heavily on the Bible and have quoted profusely from St. Paul on this matter. Women heavily involved in liberation would probably not be at home in this coalition.

In 1968, in the South, George Wallace secured 52% of the vote of members of union households, and he did very well in the rural South. These people should be the backbone of the South's contribution to a new party stressing cultural conservatism. The union members will be a generation removed from the men who sometimes lived hazardous lives in the late 1930s in order to organize the union. They should not be thought of as particularly low-income people. Their problem will be getting two cars plus their boat with an outboard motor in a two-car carport. They enjoy gospel singing, fishing, and subscribe to the notion of my-country-right-or-wrong. In general, they are disdainful of ecology and prefer economic development and the consequent creation of new jobs to any concern for the preservation of the environment. Their only reservation here is based on the adverse effect on fishing of too much water pollution. They are cool toward consumerism; it is rather too intellectual an idea. After all, they are somewhat reserved in their enthusiasm for education. A concern for education developed among Yankees who were snowbound for many months of the winter and had nothing to do but read books. Anyone who has enjoyed the mild and open winters of the South will realize the lack of stimulus to education that they provide.

But this new coalition will consist not only of Wallace followers. Business people of *new* wealth chiefly in the South and West should flock to this coalition. In fact, almost all the new Republicans of the South should be at home here in a region where industrialization is still maturing. The stress should be on the newness of the wealth. This will be the wealth of self-made men who used to walk barefoot on the old family acreage before oil was discovered under it. Outside the South this coalition should have an excellent chance of attracting

Catholics and Catholic ethnics for reasons indicated earlier. And all blue-collar and union people from genuinely poor people up to prosperous plumbers might be attracted because of fear of blacks or disapproval of the life style and values of the opposition. It would be improper to suggest that there will be perfect policy agreement among all elements of this coalition. Newly prosperous wealthy will have to recognize that unions are very much around here to stay. Although the less prosperous folk in the coalition will have relatively few demands on government (because government has already given them the basic things they need such as union security) they may still want some such type of government aid as health insurance and nursing homes. Yet all elements will be united in their opposition to affirmative action hiring of blacks and to any other form of special aid to blacks.

A great dilemma of this coalition will be to find suitable leadership. Granted that some persons with an aristocratic background like Franklin Roosevelt related well to the common man, but he was an exception. The requirement would be a person midway between the urbanity of Senator Hugh Scott of Pennsylvania and one with the earthy appeal of George Wallace. He must not project a country club image; on the other hand, he must be able to sell himself to a majority of the population in states outside the Deep South.

It would be a little unfair to the new elite to insist that all their values are the exact opposite of those enumerated. Whereas they have a more permissive attitude toward abortion, they come from areas with a much lower rate of infant mortality. The new coalition would presumably be made up of the rapidly growing knowledge industry and practically all American blacks, two groups which in some cases may overlap. Whereas the conservative coalition would certainly treat blacks with benign neglect, the knowledge industry would presumably continue in its optimistic belief that an improved standard of living and more equal distribution of wealth may be achieved through research and governmental activity. Cosmopolitanism will be greater, and there will be less acceptance of the my-country-right-or-wrong attitude. Women deeply dedicated to liberation would feel more at home in this coalition, but the great majority of women will probably feel the cross-pressures of class, race, and region.

In stressing the cultural character of this conflict, it may not be too imaginative to contemplate the young business executive who stops to see a showing of *Deep Throat* before going home to smoke a joint of marijuana. At least this emphasis on the cultural nature of the conflict may permit people who have long been economic conservatives to join with the new elite in the knowledge industry. Many of the economic issues are now moot. The business people and the knowledge industry types have come up through the same universities, and they are able to think in terms of abstractions. They both revere computers, and in other respects they are able to communicate and understand each other's language.

The Democratic Nominating Convention of 1972 was a living manifestation of pretty much this coalition, and it reflected the values discussed here. The fact that one such convention occurred most certainly does not prove that it will reoccur and produce an enduring realignment along these lines. Yet the fact that it could and did occur once certainly removes the foregoing comments from the realm of political science fiction. Because of the weakening of party loyalties, the presidential nomination is up for grabs by any such self-conscious group. Also the 1972 convention stresses the importance of noneconomic forces that politicians will have to deal with in putting together any future winning coalition, and it warns us against the danger of interpreting politics in any purely economic terms.

Five

ALIENATION: OR IS IT

MERELY PARTY DISINTEGRATION?

The preceding four chapters have recounted changes that have taken place or may take place within the American political system. Even so far-reaching a change as a realignment would be a change entirely within the present system. A different situation would present itself if a large percent of Americans lost confidence in their ability to have an impact on the political system and to make it produce results high on their scale of values. When such an event occurred, Americans could be said to be alienated from their political system. Widespread and long-continuing alienation would be perilous to our institutions. If only a handful of Americans believe that their government is honest and attentive to their wants, the basis of support for that government has been dangerously eroded.

The idea of alienation has a venerable history. It appears in the writings of Karl Marx, and it has long been used in theology in the sense of man being alienated from God. However, the now common use of the expression in the social sciences is of much more recent origin. For instance, it is noteworthy that the 1930 edition of the *Encyclopaedia of the Social Sciences* did not even carry the entry "alienation."[1] If any significant amount of alienation existed at that time or in the immediately succeeding decades, social scientists were unaware of it. Of course, politicians were viewed with profound suspicion, and over a period of years George Gallup found that six or seven out of every ten American parents did not want their children to grow up to be politicians. Yet common observation has suggested that Americans take pride in their basic political institutions. This popular impression has received some support from social scientists. Probably the most quoted single finding in Almond and Verba's *The Civic Culture* was the answer of Americans to the question, "Speaking generally, what are the things about this country that you are most proud of?" This question, directed also at respondents in four other countries, was completely open-ended. A respondent could have asserted that his greatest source of pride in his country was the beauty of its women or the grandeur of its scenery. Yet 85 percent of Americans volunteered that their greatest source of pride was in the governmental and political institutions of the United States. Britishers came in a poor second with only 46 percent making a comparable answer.[2]

By the middle 1960s and early 1970s it became apparent that Americans were losing some of their enthusiasm for their institutions. They were no longer certain that theirs was "one nation indivisible with liberty and justice for all." Political scientists eventually began to study this phenomenon. While there is no occasion to attempt an exhaustive bibliography of the subject, we can profitably review some early investigations. In "Political Cynicism: Measurement and Meaning,"[3] Agger used the word *cynicism* to mean approximately what later writers were to mean by *alienation*. The basis of the study was an extensive mail questionnaire which contained questions designed to measure the degree of cynicism. The questions formed a Guttman scale ranging from the most cynical to the least cynical. The authors found that Republicans and Democrats showed no difference in the degree of cynicism. The most cynical were persons with lowest income and least education. When education was held constant, there were only small variations in degrees of cynicism based on income. Apparently the amount of education was the most powerful factor in predicting cynicism. There was found some relationship between age and cynicism at each educational level. Persons under 35 were the most trusting, whereas graybeards 55 and over were the most cynical. It is interesting to note that this study appearing in 1961 sounds no note of alarm. The author has an interest in what he calls political cynicism, but he sees no menace to the future of the Republic.

By 1970 an effort was made to clarify the meaning of the concept *alienation*.[4] Noting that there "has emerged in this country a radical questioning and rejection of established political institutions unparalleled since the Civil War in its intensity and scope," Finifter noted four ways that alienation may be expressed.

One of these is a sense of powerlessness. The individual feels he can have no effect on public policy. A second is meaninglessness; the political decisions that are made make no sense to the citizen. By contrast even a powerless citizen may grasp the implication of a policy on which he is unable to have an effect. A third facet is normlessness—the belief that all socially accepted rules or norms are widely violated. All politicians are crooks. Watergate was unique only in that a lot of people got caught. A final category is political isolation. Here the citizen rejects the governmental norms. This is not merely a case of the Constitution being violated by conscienceless men: the Constitution itself is a fraud and a sham.

It is impossible in a short compass to summarize

fairly the author's conclusions. Finifter explores briefly the impact of each of these several facets of alienation on political behavior, but sounds no note of warning. In the real world, powerlessness may lessen turbulence and contribute to the maintenance of order. And normlessness may possibly have the effect of making a society rethink its professed ideals and try more nearly to approximate them. Reformers with a basic faith in the regime's ideals may rise up and throw the rascals out.

In "Alienation and Political Behavior," Joel D. Aberbach[5] makes a more determined effort to explore the impact of alienation on actual political behavior. Is alienation merely something that political scientists may measure as a hobby, or does alienation have a measurable impact on the real world? The author refers to studies of the relation between feelings of alienation and the defeat of referenda on drinking water fluoridation in various cities, noting that indicators of powerlessness and meaninglessness discriminated the opponents of fluoridation from its proponents. However, measurements of distrust of government did not. When he directed his attention to the 1964 presidential election, he concluded that feelings of powerlessness depress voter turnout but have no effect on which candidate the voter chooses.

More recent writers on alienation view the subject with more disquiet. They agree that over the last decade or so there has been a measurable decrease in trust in government and the consequent

impressive increase in the degree of alienation, yet
some dispute remains as to the danger inherent in
this increased alienation. Is it an unfortunate but
relatively harmless increase in griping, or is it a
decline in the degree of faith necessary to make our
institutions endure? The following remarks draw
heavily on a paper entitled "Social Conflict and
Political Estrangement, 1958–1972."[6] Professor
Miller sets forth additional ideas on the same subject in an *American Political Science Review* article,
entitled "Trust in Government."[7] The major thrust
of Miller's argument is that we have had a substantial increase in alienation over a considerable
period of time and that this is not a matter to be
taken lightly. Miller introduces the concept of political *estrangement* to avoid being bound by the defi-
nitions used by earlier writers. He sets up a scale
which incorporates some of these earlier ideas. "An
individual who believes that government wastes
the taxes ... who thinks that political leaders no
longer have the know-how or desire to make government function in a manner which will benefit
most of the people, who sees politics as increasingly
corrupt ... , and who generally feels that government is not to be trusted can be said to be politically
cynical and estranged from the government and,
presumably, the political system."[8] So one's
psychological orientation toward the government
may range from highly positive or trusting to very
negative or distrusting and cynical.

Miller believes that the ideal type of longitudinal study would be a panel study, that is, a given group of individuals would be interviewed at regular intervals over perhaps a decade to see what change has occurred in their attitude toward government. Since such panel data is unavailable, the best alternative is the use of answers to the same questions propounded to respondents over the period 1958–1972 by the Survey Research Center of the University of Michigan. The five questions as used by Miller are presented below with what is taken to be the *distrustful* or *cynical* response.[9] Miller constructs a Guttman scale on the basis of the answers to these questions.

1. How much of the time do you think you can trust the government in Washington to do what is right—just about always, most of the time, or *only some of the time?*
2. Would you say that the government is pretty much run by a *few big interests* looking out for themselves or that it is run for the benefit of all the people?
3. Do you think that people in the government waste *a lot of the money* we pay in taxes, waste some of it, or don't waste very much of it?
4. Do you feel that almost all of the people running the government are smart people who usually know what they are doing, or do you think that *quite a few of them don't seem to know what they are doing?*

5. Do you think that *quite a few* of the people running the government are a little crooked, not
many are, or do you think hardly any of them are
crooked at all?

The first conclusion is that there has been an
increase in the percent of the total population giving
cynical responses to all five trust-in-government
items. The waste-taxes item began high in 1958 and
increased dramatically through 1972. The crooked-
leaders line has wavered somewhat but shows a
slight net increase between 1958 and 1972. On the
other three items the most trusting year was 1964;
the degree of distrust began to increase thereafter.

This finding begs the next question: who is unhappy? Are all elements of the population equally
estranged, or are there one or several large groups of
the population that are peculiarly distrustful of
their government? The latter approach would
suggest a social-conflict hypothesis. One group is
doing well and feels that it lives under the best
possible government; other groups are doing poorly
and see little merit in a government under which
they get so few of the good things in life. Miller
develops an index by subtracting the percentage of
any group who have the most cynical scores (on a
Guttman scale ranging from 0 to 5) from the percentage of the group with the most trusting scores.
The most cynical scores then are numerals 4 + 5 and
the most trusting scores are 0 + 1. The resulting
percentage difference gives the preponderance of

one type of response over another. Negative index values indicate a preponderance of cynical responses over trusting responses.

The first test of this procedure is applied to racial differences. It is not surprising that blacks are considerably more cynical than whites. However, the pattern is not so simple as that statement might indicate. Among whites there has been a slow, even decline in their support index from 1958 through 1972. In this later year, their index score remains just within the positive index value. In 1958 blacks and whites had identical support-index values. By 1964 black support had actually increased somewhat. By 1968 it had registered a substantial decline, and between 1968 and 1972 the decline in support was so sharp and dramatic that it nearly came off the bottom of the graph. In that year blacks had a negative index value and were clearly more estranged than whites.

Estrangement values are next examined in terms of income, with separate treatments for whites and blacks. Among whites several interesting conclusions emerged. In 1958 the most prosperous of the four income categories was the most trusting, but the differences among the groups were not impressive. Between 1958 and 1972 there was a decline in trust of major proportions for all four income groups. In 1972, however, the high and the medium-high income groups—in that order—remained the relatively most trusting.

The pattern for blacks is more complex. In 1958,

1964, and 1968, blacks were more trusting than their white counterparts. But between 1968 and 1972 the very bottom of the trust market dropped out for blacks. All groups of the black population ended up in 1972 infinitely more distrustful than any group of whites, and the medium-high group was the most distrustful within the black community.

Class status may also be analyzed by dividing both the white population and the black population into professional, gray collar, blue collar, and farmers. The results for both black and white are essentially the same as those produced by an analysis of income. All groups of the population registered a decline in political trust over the fourteen-year period. In the white community in 1958 the most trusting were those in the most prestigious occupations, but even among professional people there was a startling decline in trust between 1958 and 1972. Blacks were again relatively more trusting than whites in 1964, but between 1968 and 1972 they registered an awesome and dramatic increase in their distrust of government.

The test for subjective class status was next raised: Do you regard yourself as a member of the working class or of the middle class? Finally, there is a question about whether the respondent regards himself as having been upwardly mobile, downwardly mobile, or remaining stationary. The general conclusion is that whites with a good income and social position and a record of upward mobility are to some degree more supportive of the government than those less fortunately situated. However, this is merely a relative statement. The fact that these population categories would seem to have it made has not precluded their developing over a fourteen-year period an impressive degree of political estrangement. With blacks the picture is similar through 1968, but between then and 1972 there seems to have developed a united front of black political disenchantment. Prosperous blacks have joined their poorer brethren in a phenomenon of extreme political disenchantment.

Age differences related to political estrangement in a complex manner. The problem is illustrated by the fact that persons over 50 are more politically estranged than somewhat younger individuals. This raises the question whether all voters become more cynical as they grow older or whether the life experiences of certain age cohorts incline them to greater cynicism. While distrust among the older group is attributed by Miller to the aging process, the estrangement of the young is attributed to the unique experiences of their generation. In any event, age-related differences in political support "were found to be emerging between youth and middle-aged groups ... at the same time, distrust was deepening among the oldest age groups."[10]

Finally, Miller makes an effort to isolate the aspect of American government that elicits the greatest degree of distrust. The questions designed to call forth the appropriate responses are:

1. How much do you feel that political parties help to make the government pay attention to what people think: a great deal, some, or not much?
2. And how much do you feel that having elections makes the government pay attention to what people think: a good deal, some, or not much?
3. How much attention do you think Congressmen pay to the people who elect them when they decide what to do in Congress? A great deal, some, or not much?

Americans, it turns out, have more confidence in elections than either their parties or their congressmen. The difference is substantial. However, trust has declined on all three items for both races. For blacks the declining trust in parties and congressmen is uniform and precipitate from 1964 through 1972. Their skepticism about elections began in 1968. On all three items, the declining faith of whites has been less but still substantial.

The remaining fundamental question is whether these distrustful attitudes have any effect on political behavior in the real world. This is the substance of the clash of views between Professors Citrin and Miller alluded to in footnote 7. One cannot compress Professor Citrin's scholarship into a sentence or two, but he is not persuaded that the negative attitudes uncovered by Miller are a cause for alarm. He attempts to show by a re-reading of Miller's own data that Americans retain considerable faith in their government. More basically, he argues that responses to public opinion poll questions have little predictive value for political behavior or changes in political behavior. He notes that American baseball fans may shout "Kill the umpire," yet few umpires have died at the hands of enraged fans. In short, responses to polls may constitute rhetoric that need not drive us to despair about the future of American institutions.

Miller will have none of this line of reasoning. In his rejoinder, he seeks to demonstrate that lack of trust has already had a demonstrable impact on political behavior. He begins by noting that there is a coincidence in time between the decline in presidential voting and the decline in political trust. "Turnout has been dropping since 1960; 1972 witnessed the lowest turnout of any presidential election since 1948."[11] Obviously this temporal coincidence is merely suggestive. What must be demonstrated is a degree of political estrangement on the part of the non-voters as compared with voters in presidential elections. This indeed turns out to be the case. Whereas in 1958 there was an almost identical degree of political trust among both voters and non-voters, in the following three elections, voters were markedly more supportive than non-voters.

It is a reasonable guess that political discontent has been directed at the parties. If so, a reasonable hypothesis is that political estrangement may be related to relatively weaker partisan attachment. Individuals with the weakest partisan attachment should be the most distrusting of government whereas strong identifiers may be hypothesized as having greater faith in it. In 1958, this hypothesis was wholly without support; the strong identifiers were the least trusting whereas leaners, independents, and weak identifiers were considerably more trusting. In the 1964 and 1968 elections a linear relationship did prevail, with trust being greatest among the strong identifiers and least among the independents. By 1972 an odd curvilinear relationship appeared with strong identifiers and independents being less trusting than either weak identifiers or leaners.[12] So this data hardly offers a strong confirmation of the hypothesis.

If there is added to the idea of trust the concept of political efficacy (the individual's faith that his vote counts and that he can have an impact on his government) one finds that in the 1972 presidential election there was an 89 percent turnout among those who were trusting and felt efficacious while among those who felt both inefficacious and distrusting only 62 percent voted.[13] Moreover, trusting versus cynical attitudes toward government are conditioned by a voter's ideology—whether he is disposed more toward social change or more toward social control. At least, this relationship may be demonstrated if one is willing to accept a respondent's reply to a question about willingness to participate in unconventional forms of political activity as being the equivalent of political behavior. The Miller article deals with respondents' answers to questions about willingness to engage in a legal protest march, a refusal to obey unjust laws, and willingness to participate in disruptive sit-ins and demonstrations. When one controls cynicism and trust and compares respondents with a social-change versus a so-called social-control ideology, it appears not only that all cynics are more approving of unconventional political behavior but that cynics with a social-change ideology are much more approving of unconventional political behavior than even their social-control counterparts.

The foregoing arguments seek to demonstrate that there is considerable evidence of a relationship between an attitude of political alienation and political behavior. Yet we are left completely in the dark as to what forms of political behavior are evoked by alienation. After all this lengthy and polysyllabic discourse, it seems anticlimactic and unoriginal to allude again to a party realignment. Yet the absence of trust in the present parties (as well as the prevailing mistrust for the entire political system) suggests that vast numbers of Americans might be receptive to a party realignment. Or one might infer with equal logic that multitudes of Americans are looking for a new political messiah. Yet is this to be a messiah with a sword and private armies or a messiah within the framework of our inherited political system? On this point most of our current research provides no answer.

One writer who shows little trepidation in predicting the impact of alienation on political behavior is David C. Schwartz. In his *Political Aliena-*

tion and Political Behavior,[14] Schwartz has developed a theory of political alienation and then submitted his theory to a series of empirical tests between the spring of 1968 and the spring of 1970. He uses for his tests a city-wide sample of Newark, New Jersey, and a variety of different class and racial groups in Philadelphia. Also studies were conducted of the student population of several universities. The author finds very substantial amounts of alienation in all these communities. He finds, too, a widespread willingness to engage in unconventional political behavior. In fact, a reader comes away with the impression that few Americans are really giving serious consideration to using the conventional political machinery to improve their lot. Moreover, he finds that alienation leads not to apathy but to a search for new solutions and to essentially revolutionary approaches. The word *revolutionary* is used carelessly here and does not designate a well-organized Marxist conspiracy.

The book is challenging and intellectually stimulating. Yet it seems incredibly dated. The attitudes and violent actions so faithfully reflected in the data collected during 1968–1970 now seem a thing of the past. The reactions of his respondents to the events of that era may be intellectually valid and practically important if such a situation ever recurs. We do not really know why the ghetto riots have subsided although we may presume that campus riots have ended as a result of the end of the draft and the end of the Vietnamese War. Yet the overall impression from the study is that of an author with a considerable enterprise and intellectual vigor who has written a challenging study of a vanished era. Possibly the explanation of the unforeseen change is a matter of age cohorts. We had at that time an excessively large number of citizens in the 14 through 24-year-old age bracket. Now an ever-increasing percentage of that cohort has gotten beyond 24, become employed, married, and started to make payments on a house and car. The number of persons now emerging in the most troublemaking period of their lives is substantially less than was true slightly less than a decade ago.

Nor have the alienated constituted a unified group capable of following the banner of a particular leader. Seven or eight years ago it was fashionable to write about Alabama Governor George C. Wallace as a possible leader of the most alienated. But now it seems that this particular leader has made his last appearance on the national stage.

An alternate guess about the political behavior of the alienated is to contend that their frustration will result in ever-increasing apathy. This apathy—this complete erosion of civic competence—will lead to a growing feeling of inability to hold public officials responsible. These officials will therefore become increasingly irresponsible and corrupt because they know they can get away with it. Yet this conclusion is not too persuasive. After all, Nixon was forced out of the White House.

The weight of evidence seems to be that Americans are more alienated from their parties than from their governmental institutions. Parties are at an all-time low not only in the degree of trust that they evoke but also in their effectiveness and importance. Evidence for this statement has been recounted at length. Particular stress should be laid on the growing number of persons who identify themselves as independents. Equally important is the decline of party identification as a predictive factor in how a person will vote in contrast to the rise of issues as a predictive factor. Important, too, is split-level voting. No writers have offered a persuasive explanation as to why an increasing number of Americans support the candidate of one party for president and that of the other party for congressman. At any rate, the widespread practice of split-level voting vitiates the very idea of party responsibility, which assumes that partisans in office will work as a team and will be judged on the basis of group performance.

All the foregoing is an interesting contrast to the American Political Science Association's *Toward a More Responsible Two-Party System*,[15] issued in 1950. This much debated publication associated an increasing degree of party discipline in Congress with a reasonably sharp differentiation between the two parties on issues. Instead we see the growth of issue consciousness coupled with the weakening of parties and a widespread apathy and disenchantment with parties. Obviously a uniform degree of apathy does not prevail among all eligible voters.

Instead we find large groups of highly issue-conscious true-believers who can be very politically active and effective. With the weakening of parties the presidential nomination is up for grabs by any such self-conscious political group.

The obvious examples of successful grabs are the capture of the Republican nomination by Goldwater in 1964 and the Democratic nomination by Senator McGovern in 1972. In both cases there was a movement in search of a candidate. Governor Ronald Reagan's surprisingly close race against President Ford in 1976 is another example of the same phenomenon. In each case a large body of issue-oriented activists worked to secure the nomination. It should be noted that the whole idea of a nomination being up for grabs by such ideologically based groups is not in harmony with the concept of a realignment. The latter assumes a new choosing up of sides and the creation of relatively durable coalitions.

Conditions have conspired to make our era one in which a high degree of alienation is likely to continue. The problem is the increased number of contenders in the political arena, all of whom have rising expectations. Miller found in his answers to every series of questions propounded that blacks were vastly more alienated than whites. Only a few years ago, as Americans measure history, no one needed to care what blacks thought or felt about any aspect of the political system. As recently as 1910, 85 percent of American blacks lived in the South and were disfranchised. As recently as 1950, 63 percent of American blacks lived in the South, and relatively few of them voted in that year. Today, blacks are very much inside the political ball park, or, to change the figure of speech, the area of conflict has spread and they are full participants in it. The politician's task of keeping everybody happy has become infinitely more difficult. Any improvement in the situation of blacks may be perceived as a threat by large numbers of whites. All the remarks applying to the black population apply with equal force to the Chicano population of the Southwest, as well as to Spanish-speaking Americans elsewhere. As recently as 1948 when Lyndon Johnson was elected U.S. senator from Texas, Chicanos (then "Mexicans") were *being voted;* now they vote. Two congressmen from Texas have Spanish surnames, as do an ever-increasing number of local officials. Chicanos do not confine themselves to making such heretical observations as that one of the defenders of the Alamo was a slave trader; instead they go on to make demands on government on behalf of their group.

The vaguely defined phenomenon of Women's Liberation is not exactly parallel to the preceding two, but it does extend the area of political conflict. This movement involves many nonpolitical aspects such as who does what proportion of the housework and child-rearing. Also, since we are talking not about a minority, but a majority, of the population it should be pointed out that women are divided by lines of class, race, religion, and ethnicity. We do not find here a monolithic sisterhood in essential agreement on their aims. Yet when all this has been said, the fact remains that women leaders are making demands on government that would have been unthinkable fifteen years ago. We cannot bring back the "good old days" when the only players in the political ball park were white males. Nor is it likely that governmental programs can be worked out that will simultaneously satisfy blacks, Chicanos, women, and all other elements of the population. If government pursues a policy beneficial to blacks, Chicanos, and women, other elements of the population will feel threatened and will fight back. There may be a lesson to be learned in the slowdown of the drive for the Equal Rights Amendment. At first the proposal sailed through a number of state legislatures with little or no opposition, but later a powerful backlash developed under the leadership of women who had a different philosophy of women's role from that held by the proponents of the Equal Rights Amendment. We live in an era when a high degree of alienation is simply built into the situation.

None of this is a counsel to relaxation or a suggestion that we are living in the best of all possible worlds. Surely if representative government is to do its job, there must be a certain minimum of trust in the governors by the governed. The entry into the political arena of new contenders will make it ever more difficult for the politicians to satisfy them without antagonizing other groups. Yet all may not be lost. The inventors of our measuring instruments have exercised commendable ingenuity, but they recognize the frailty of these instruments. Surely we have established no direct relationship between increased alienation and imminent disaster. Additional research may refine our categories of alienation and increase our ability to predict from them a particular type of political behavior. But right now the fall of the Bastille does not seem to be just around the corner.

Postscript

Although any author must eventually bring his manuscript to a conclusion and reconcile himself to the march of events that may change the picture before his study is published, we should at least note the election of Jimmy Carter. The first observation is that none of the standard studies of political behavior would have lead anyone to predict his nomination and election. Possibly the best that political scientists can do to salvage their dignity is to point out that the declining faith in government set up an ideal situation for a candidate whose experience had been entirely in state politics. With an anti-Washington mood abroad, here was a nominee uncorrupted by any contact with the capital city.

We must await a painstaking analysis by our colleagues in survey research to tell us more about who voted for Carter and why. Any suggestion that

he has revived the New Deal Coalition is meaning-
ful only when compared with the years 1968 and
1972. Polls taken by the news magazines refer to
Carter's slim majority among Catholics, ethnics,
organized labor, and blue-collar workers. Then
comparisons are made with percent of support received from these groups in earlier years. This is a
most inexact procedure which may well be counting
the same person several times as in the case of a
Catholic, blue-collar worker who belongs to a union.
And, of course, Carter won in a different South from
the one that supported Franklin Roosevelt. Carter
depended upon the overwhelming support of blacks
who could not vote in earlier decades and drew also
on lower-income and rural whites, few of whom
bothered to vote in the presidential elections of the
New Deal era.

At the time of the present writing there is no
indication that Carter's support will have the qual-
ity of permanence one associates with a realignment. The very large percentage of voters who made
up their minds in the last few weeks of the campaign
suggests that they did not believe that Carter was
championing any issues which they considered important. The contrast with the elections of 1964 and
1972 is sharp. In these elections many voters perceived the candidates as espousing or opposing their
views, and these voters decided early and adhered to
their decisions tenaciously. The loyalty of millions
of Carter voters may be described as tentative and
half-hearted.

His near-unanimous support by black voters underlines the difficulty of a politician in relation to the new entrants into the political arena. He must do something for them, or they may stay home on election day in 1980. He can give blacks the psychological reward of appointing gifted members of their race to prominent and responsible positions, but he cannot push economic programs beneficial to blacks alone without encouraging an adverse reaction on the part of majority elements of the population.

Notes

CHAPTER 1

1. Paul Lazarsfeld, Bernard Berelson, and Helen Gaudet, *The People's Choice* (New York: Columbia University Press, 1948), 178.
2. By Herbert McClosky, Paul J. Hoffman, and Rosemary O'Hara, vol. 54, 406–427.
3. Angus Campbell, Philip E. Converse, Warren E. Miller, and Donald E. Stokes, *The American Voter* (New York: Wiley and Sons, 1960), 573.
4. Bernard R. Berelson, Paul F. Lazarsfeld, and William N. McPhee, *Voting* (Chicago: University of Chicago Press, 1954), 395.

5. (Cambridge, Mass., 1966), 156.
6. Vol. 66, pp. 415–428. Pomper's ideas on issue awareness are more fully developed in his *Voters' Choice: Varieties of American Electoral Behavior* (New York: Dodd, Mead, 1975)
7. *Ibid,* p. 418.
8. *Op. cit.,* p. 421.
9. P. 69.
10. Philip E. Converse, "The Nature of Belief Systems in Mass Politics," Chapter 6 in David Apter (ed.) *Ideology and Discontent* (New York: Free Press, 1964).
11. *Public Opinion and American Democracy* (New York: Knopf, 1961).
12. Vol. 36, pp. 540–591. Nie's thought in this area is developed more fully in Norman H. Nie, Sidney Verba, and John R. Petrocik, *The Changing American Voter* (Cambridge, Mass: Harvard University Press, 1976), xxii, 399.
13. *Op. cit.*
14. *Ibid.,* p. 586

CHAPTER 2

1. (Washington, D.C.: The Brookings Institution, 1973), 388. A more somber view of the future of the party system appears in Walter Dean Burnham's *Critical Elections and the Mainsprings of American Politics* (New York: Norton, 1970).
2. *Dynamics,* p. 310.
3. *Op cit.,* p. 324.
4. Walter DeVries and Lance Tarrance, Jr., *The Ticket-Splitter: A New Force in American Politics* (Eerdmans, 1972), p. 31.

CHAPTER 3

1. These figures include the eleven states of the Confederacy plus Kentucky and Oklahoma.

2. These and subsequent polling results appear in a paper written by Raymond B. Wolfinger and Robert B. Arsenau entitled, "Partisan Change in the South," delivered at the 1974 meeting of the American Political Science Association. Data in this paragraph come from Table 5.

3. Wolfinger and Arseneau, Table 3.

4. *Op. cit.,* Table 7.

5. September 27, 1967.

6. Wolfinger and Arseneau, Table 6.

7. Norman H. Nie, "Mass Belief Systems Revisited," *Journal of Politics* 36 (August 1974), 586.

8. Nov. 15, 1976, p. 19.

9. Nov. 15, 1976, p. 19.

CHAPTER 4

1. (New Rochelle, N.Y.: Arlington House, 1969), 482.

2. (Garden City, N.Y.: Doubleday, 1975), 246.

3. *Sipuel* v. *Board of Regents of the University of Oklahoma,* 332 U.S. 631 (1948).

4. *Mediacracy,* p. 98.

5. Everett Carll Ladd with Charles D. Hadley, *Transformations of the American Party System: Political Coalitions from the New Deal to the 1970's* (New York: Norton, 1975), pp. 234–239.

6. Richard Jensen, "The Historical Roots of Party Identification" (paper presented at the 1969 meeting of the American Political Science Association, quoted in *Mediacracy*), p. 120.

7. Jensen, quoted in *Mediacracy,* pp. 126–127.

CHAPTER 5

1. "Alienation as a Concept in the Social Sciences," *Current Sociology,* Vol. XXI, 1973, Number 1, p. 9.

2. Gabriel Almond and Sidney Verba, *The Civic Culture* (Princeton: Princeton University Press, 1963), 102.

3. Robert E. Agger, *The Journal of Politics,* 23 (August 1961), 447.
4. Ada W. Finifter, "Dimensions of Political Alienation," *American Political Science Review,* LXIV (June 1970), 389–410.
5. *The American Political Science Review,* LXIII (March, 1969), 86–99.
6. A paper by Arthur H. Miller, Thad A. Brown, and Alden S. Raine prepared for delivery at the 1973 Midwest Political Science Association Convention, Chicago, May 3–5.
7. "Trust in Government," LXVIII (September 1974), 951–972. The article is followed by some critical comments by Jack Citrin (pp. 973–988), comments which call forth a spirited rejoinder by Miller, pp. 989–1001.
8. "Social Conflict," p. 3.
9. "Social Conflict," p. 4.
10. "Social Conflict," p. 61.
11. "Social Conflict," p. 65.
12. In the jargon of the trade, a *leaner* is a person who first responds that he is an independent but when pressed as to whether he leans toward one party or the other is able to name the party toward which he inclines.
13. Table 4, p. 52. *A Majority Party in Disarray: Policy Polarization in the 1972 Election* by Arthur H. Miller, Warren E. Miller, Alden S. Raine, and Thad A. Brown (University of Michigan, Center for Political Studies), Mimeographed.
14. (Chicago: Aldine Publishing Company, 1973), p. 286.
15. *American Political Science Review,* XLIV:3, Part 2, Sept. 1950.

Index